# THIS COLORING BOOK BELONGS TO:

# Color Chart

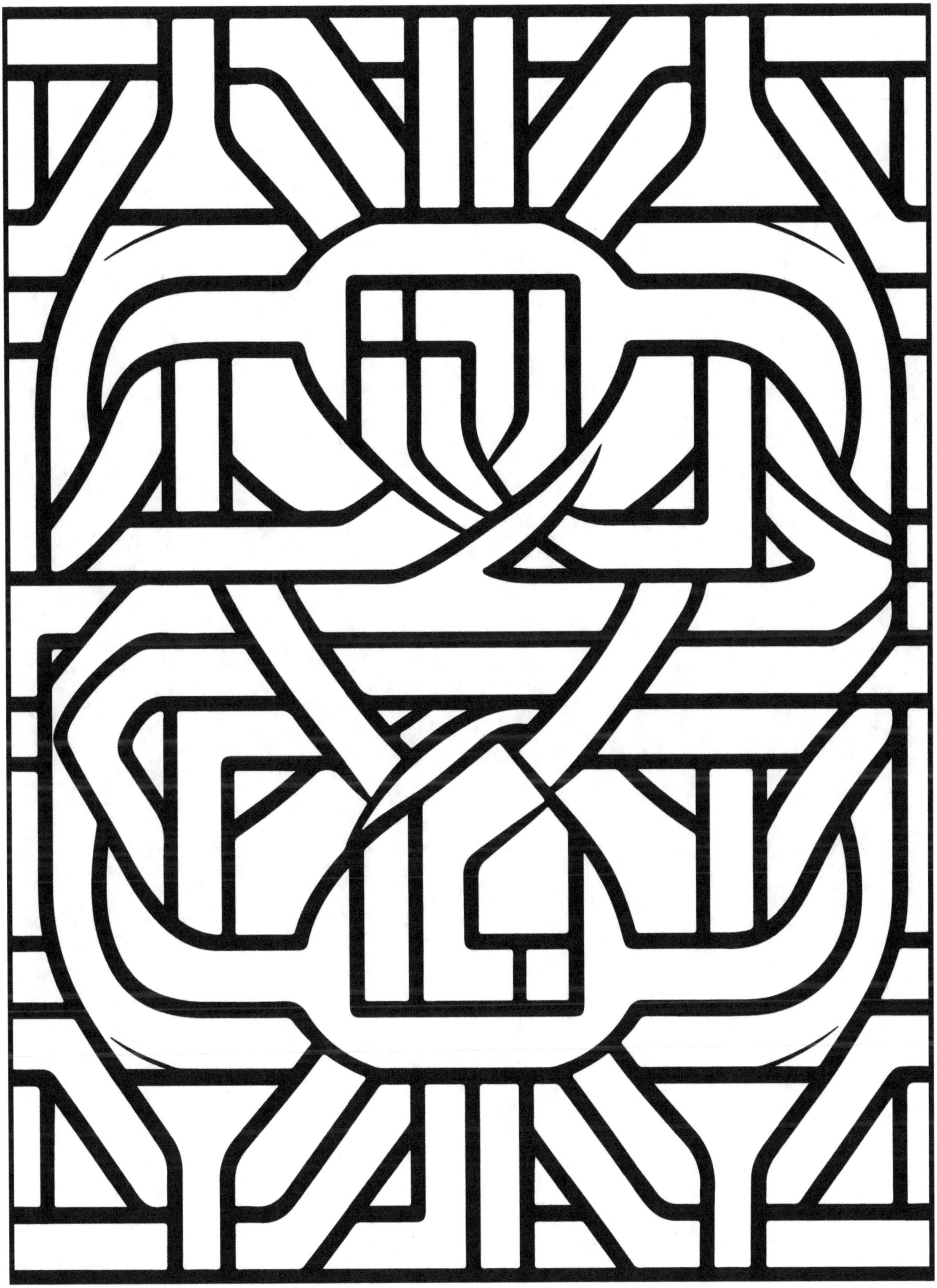

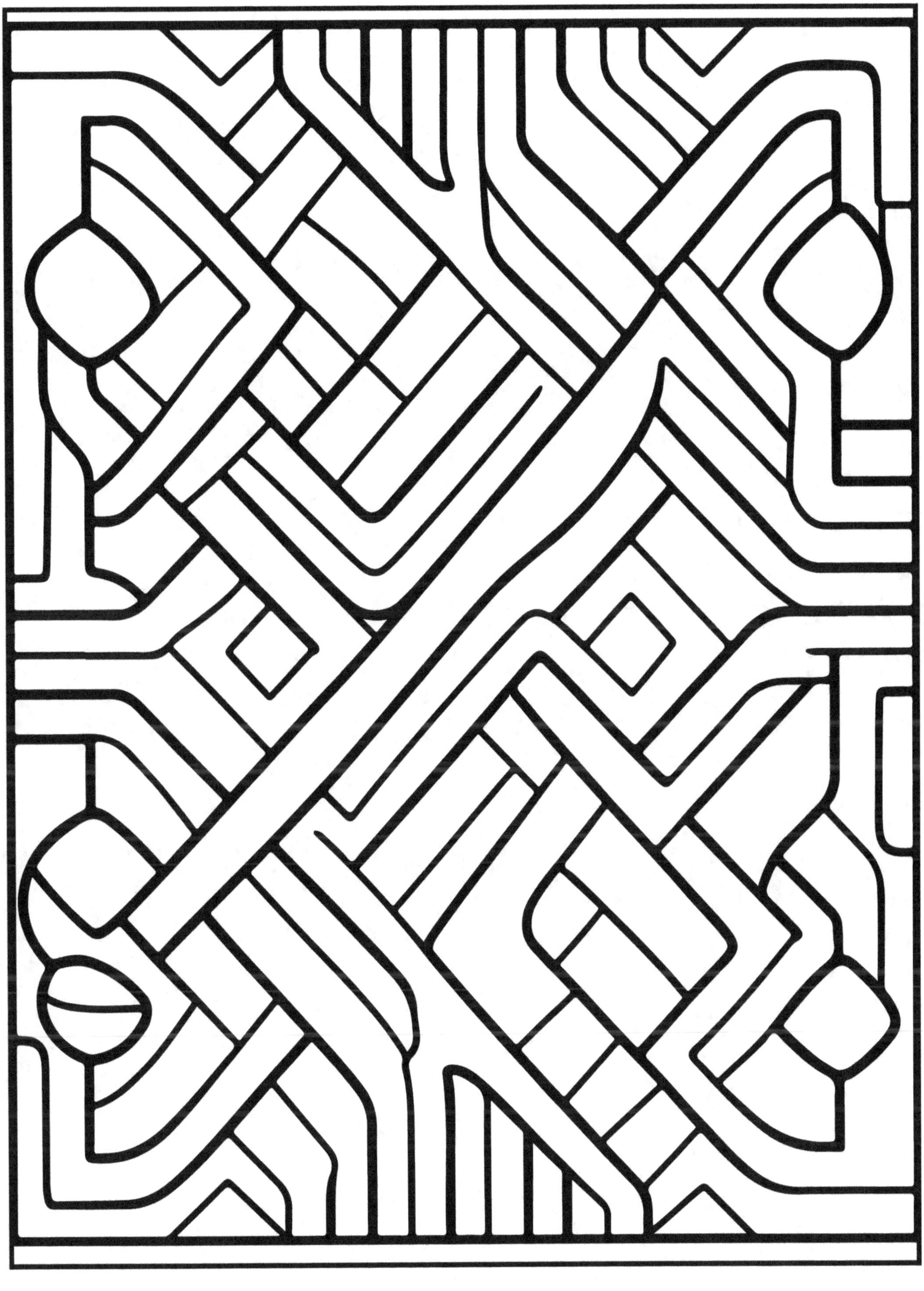

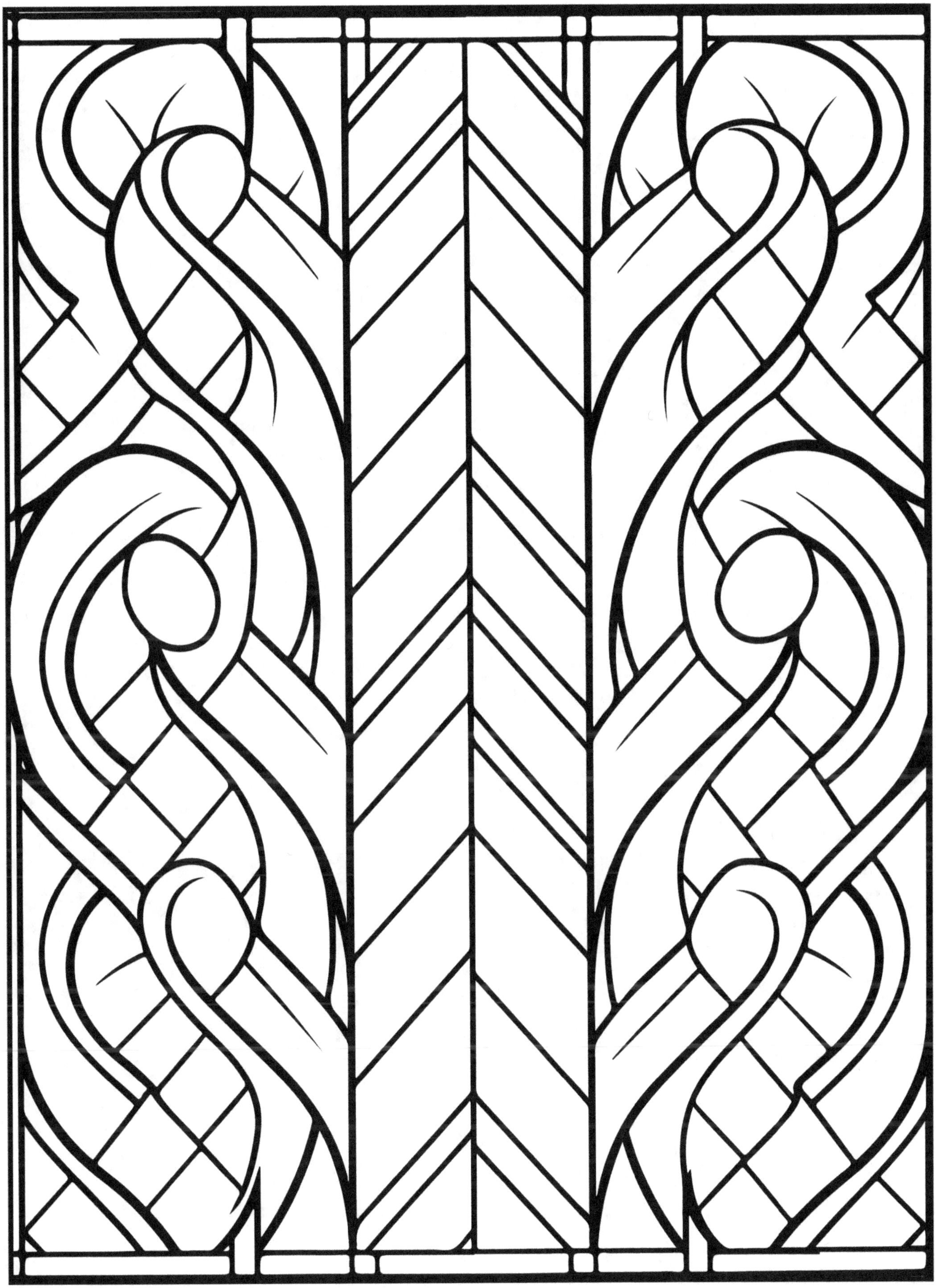

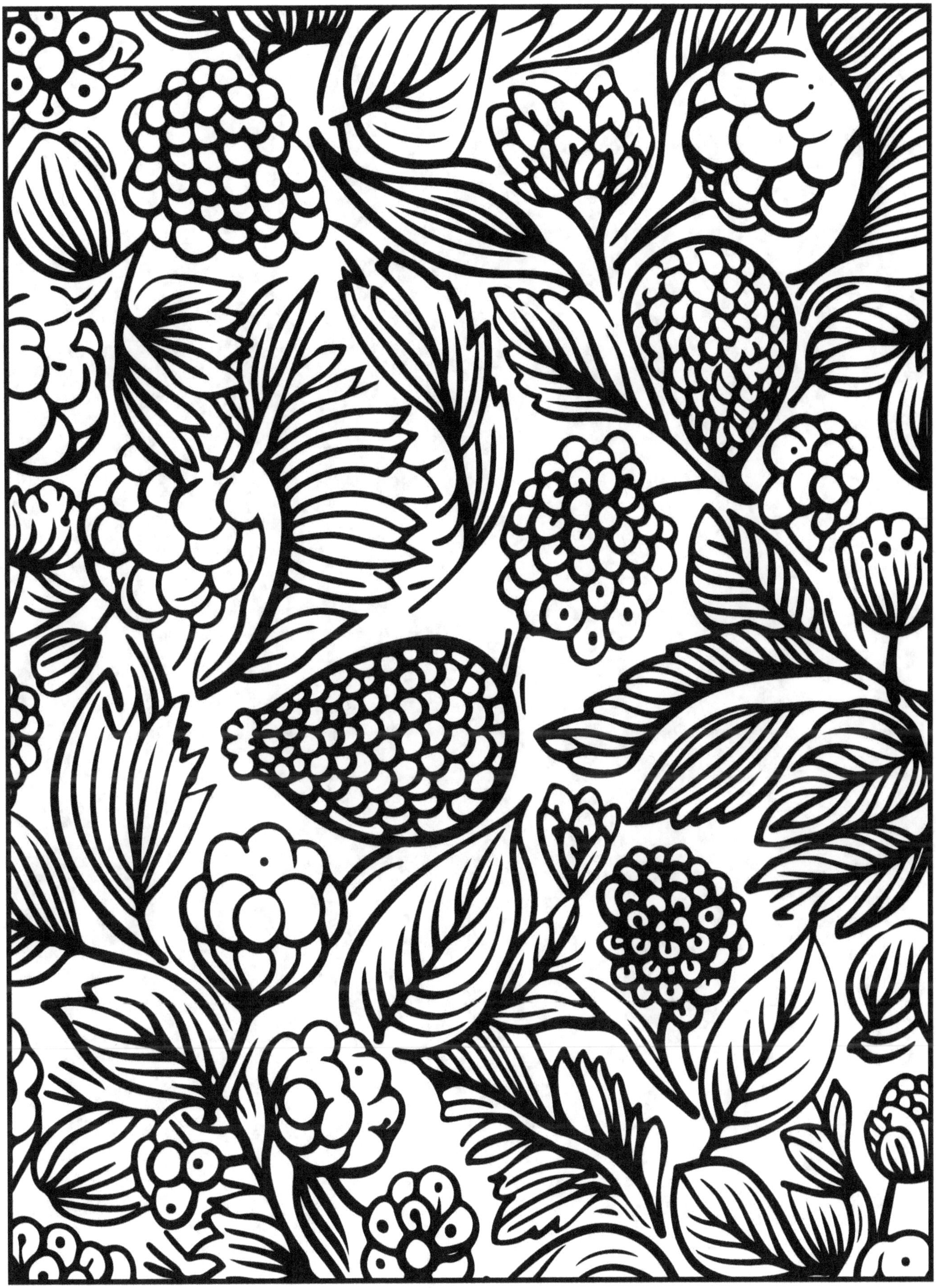

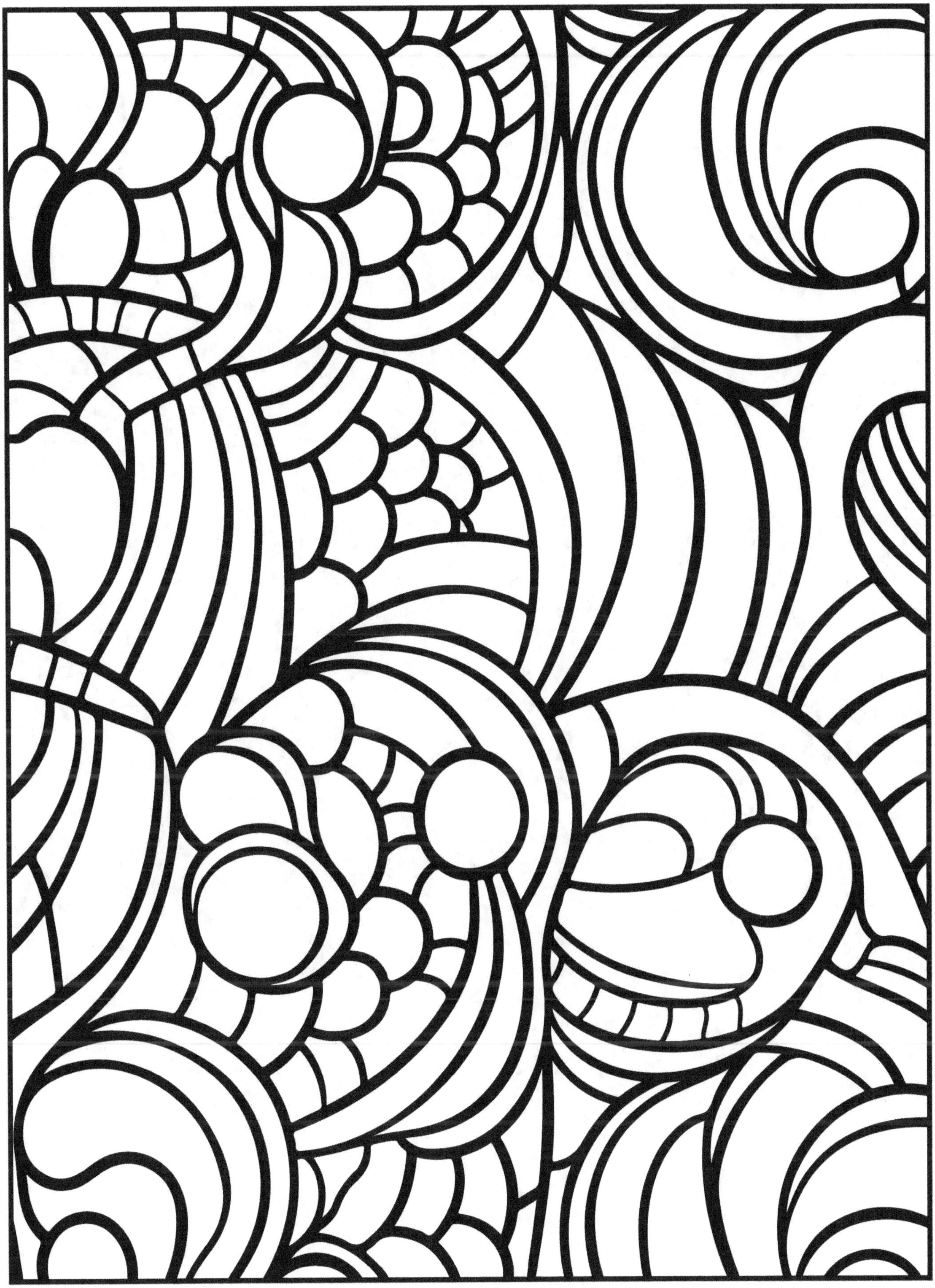

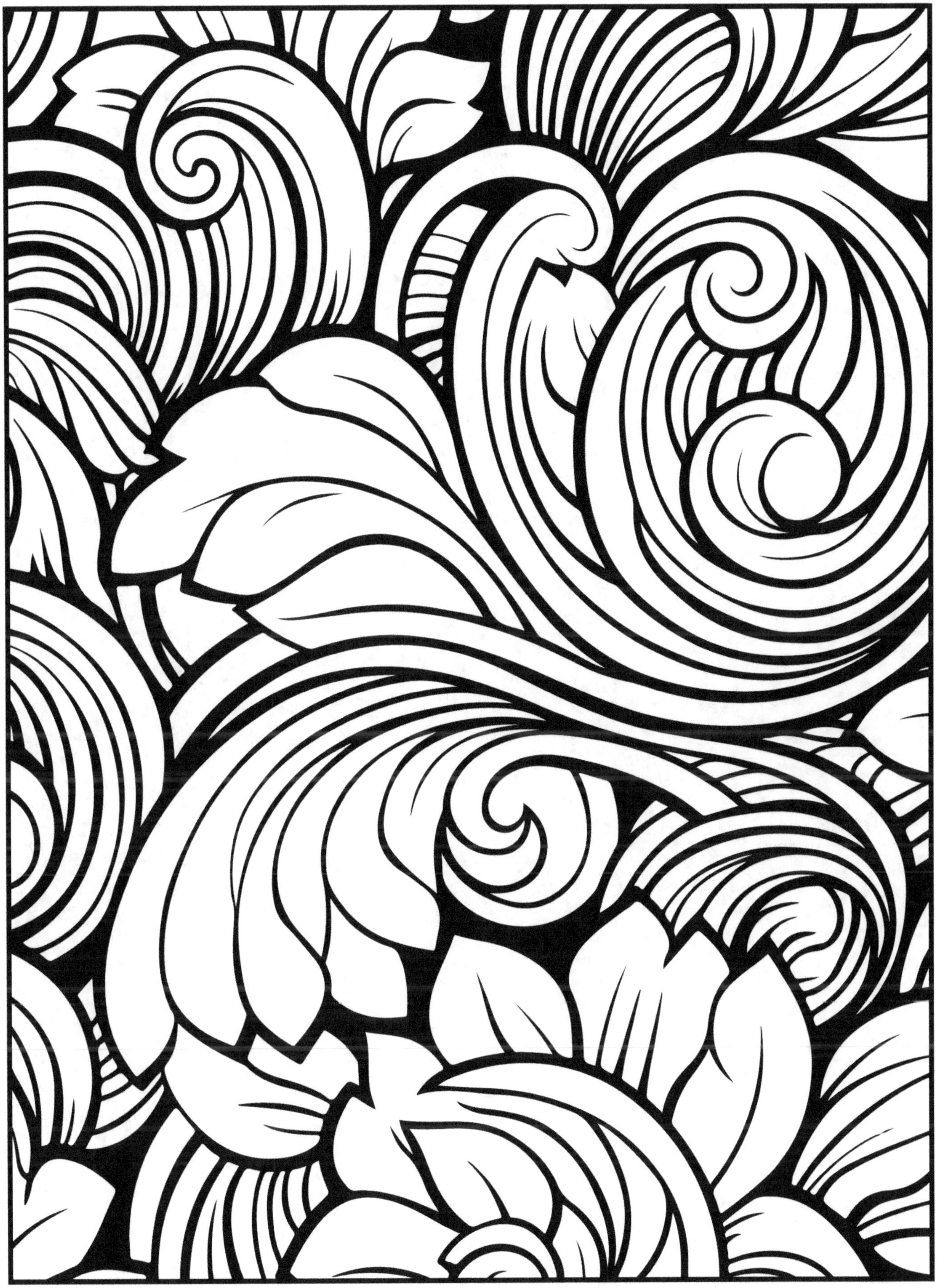

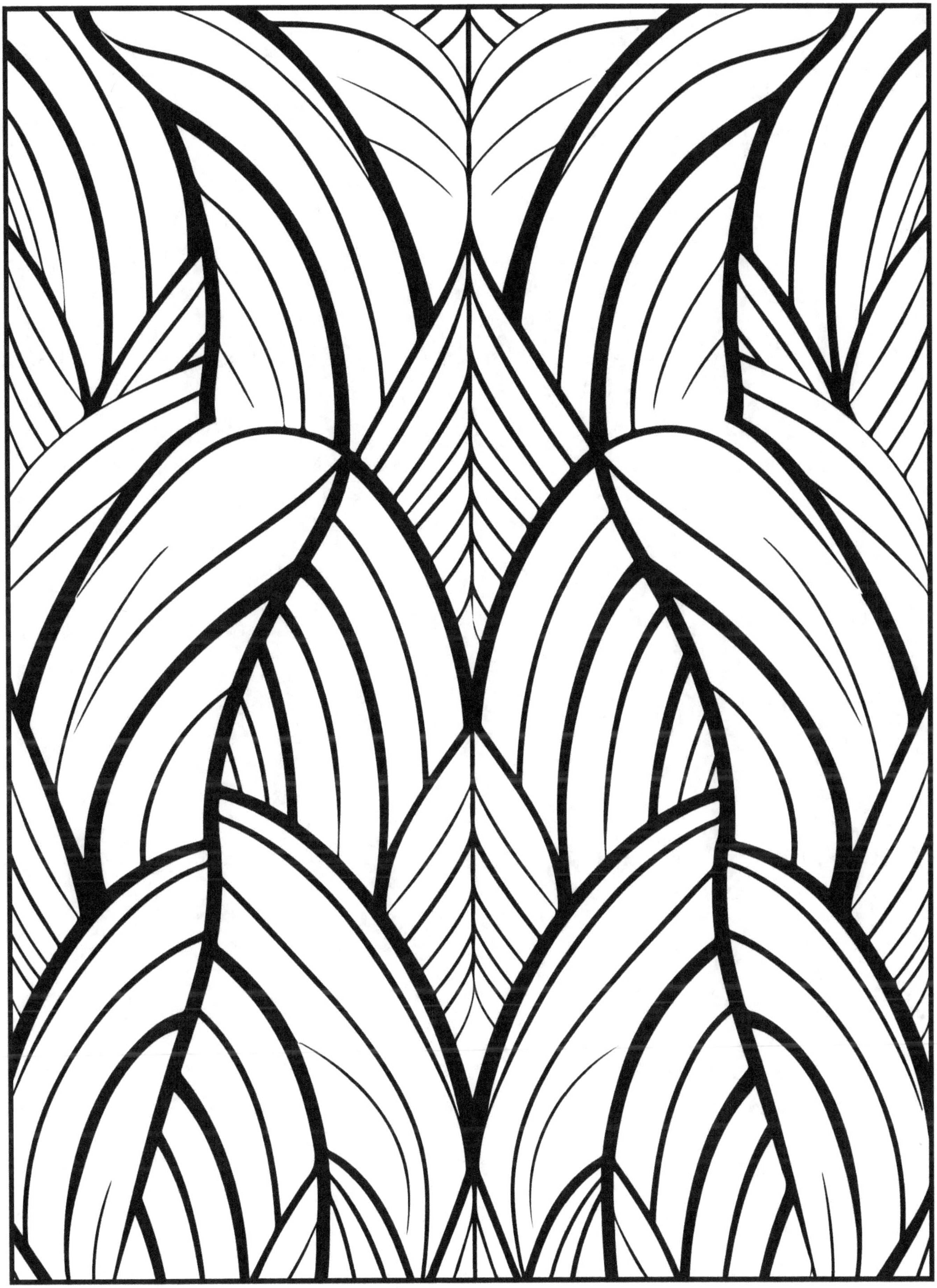

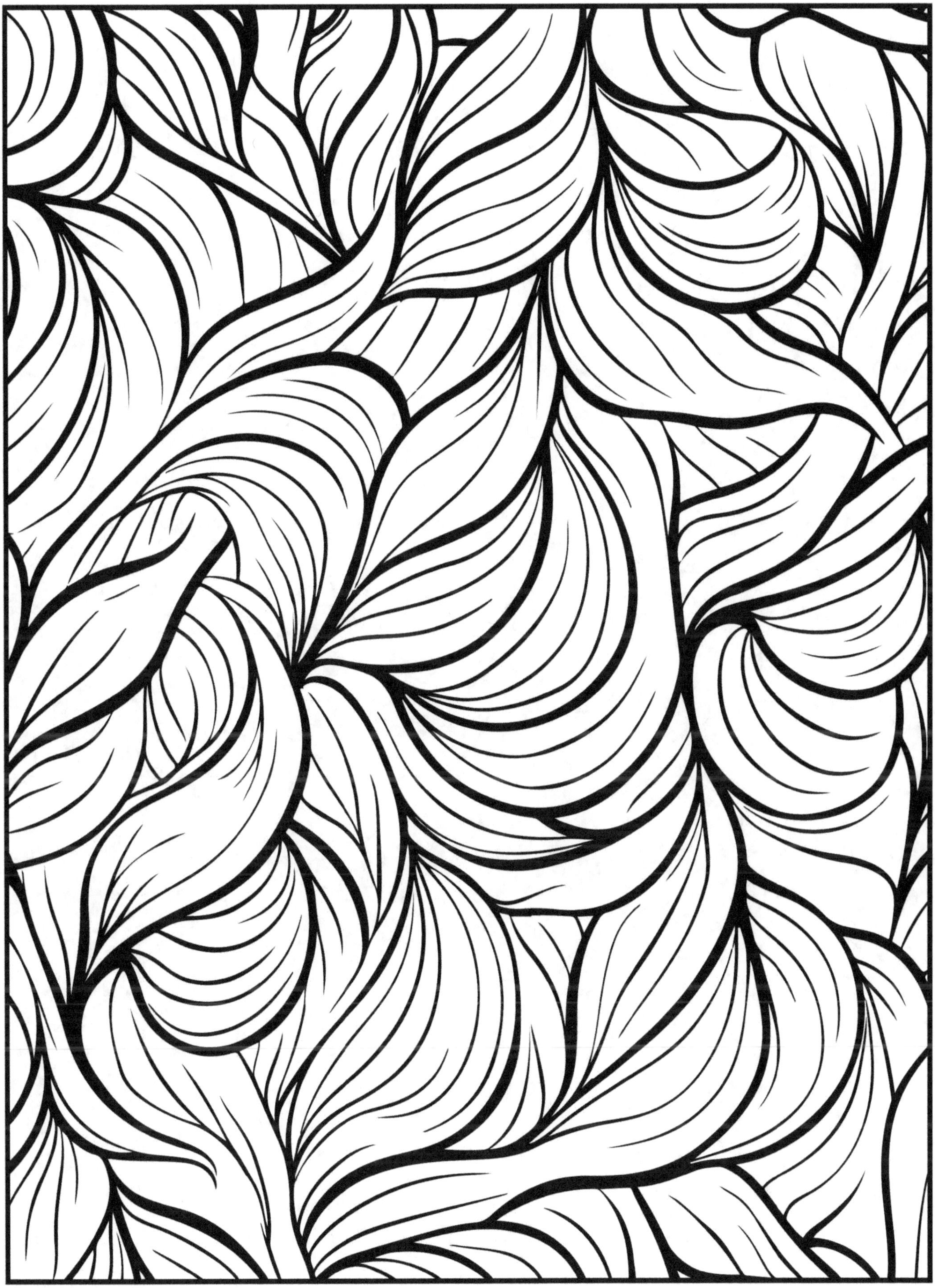

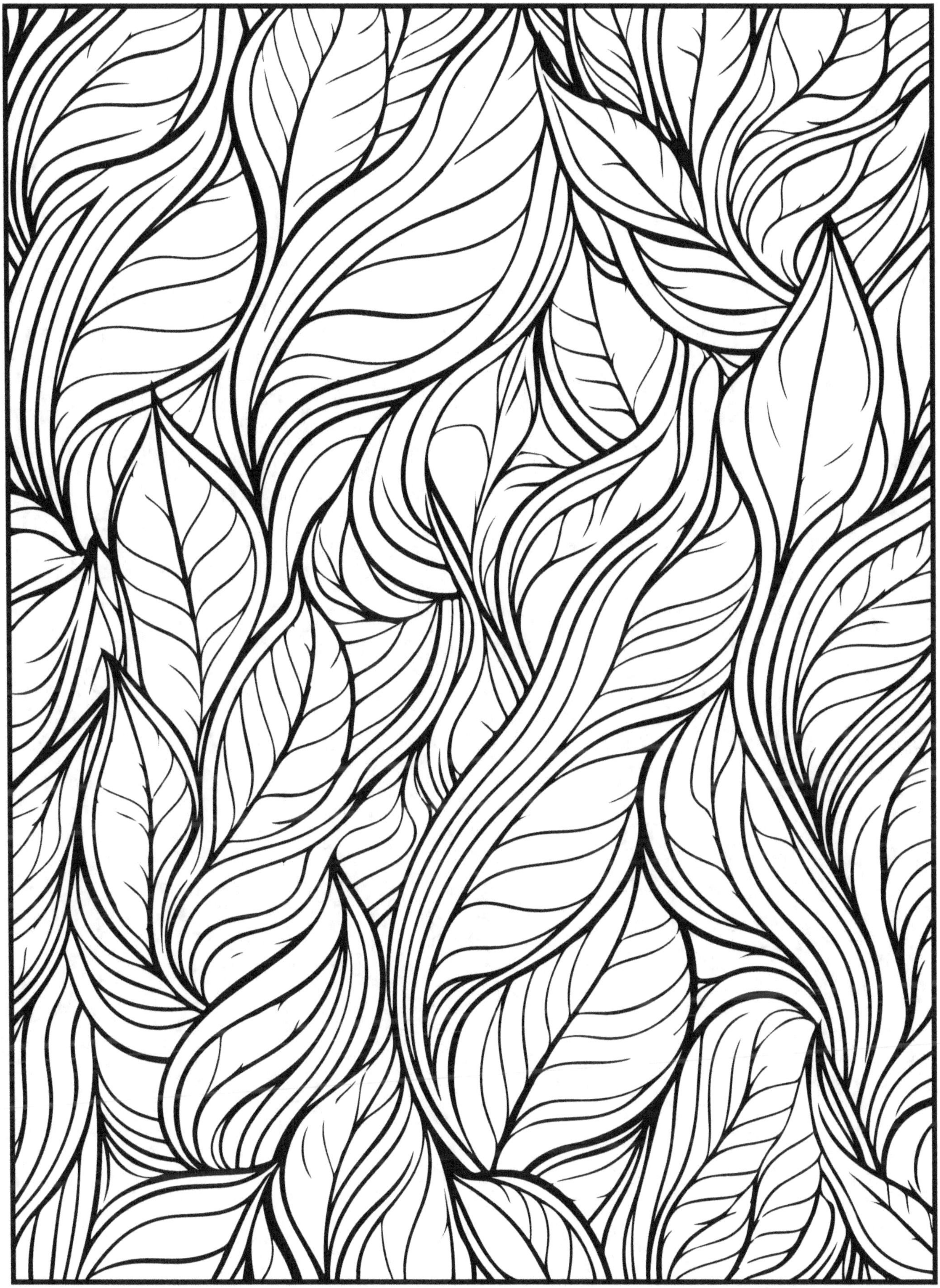

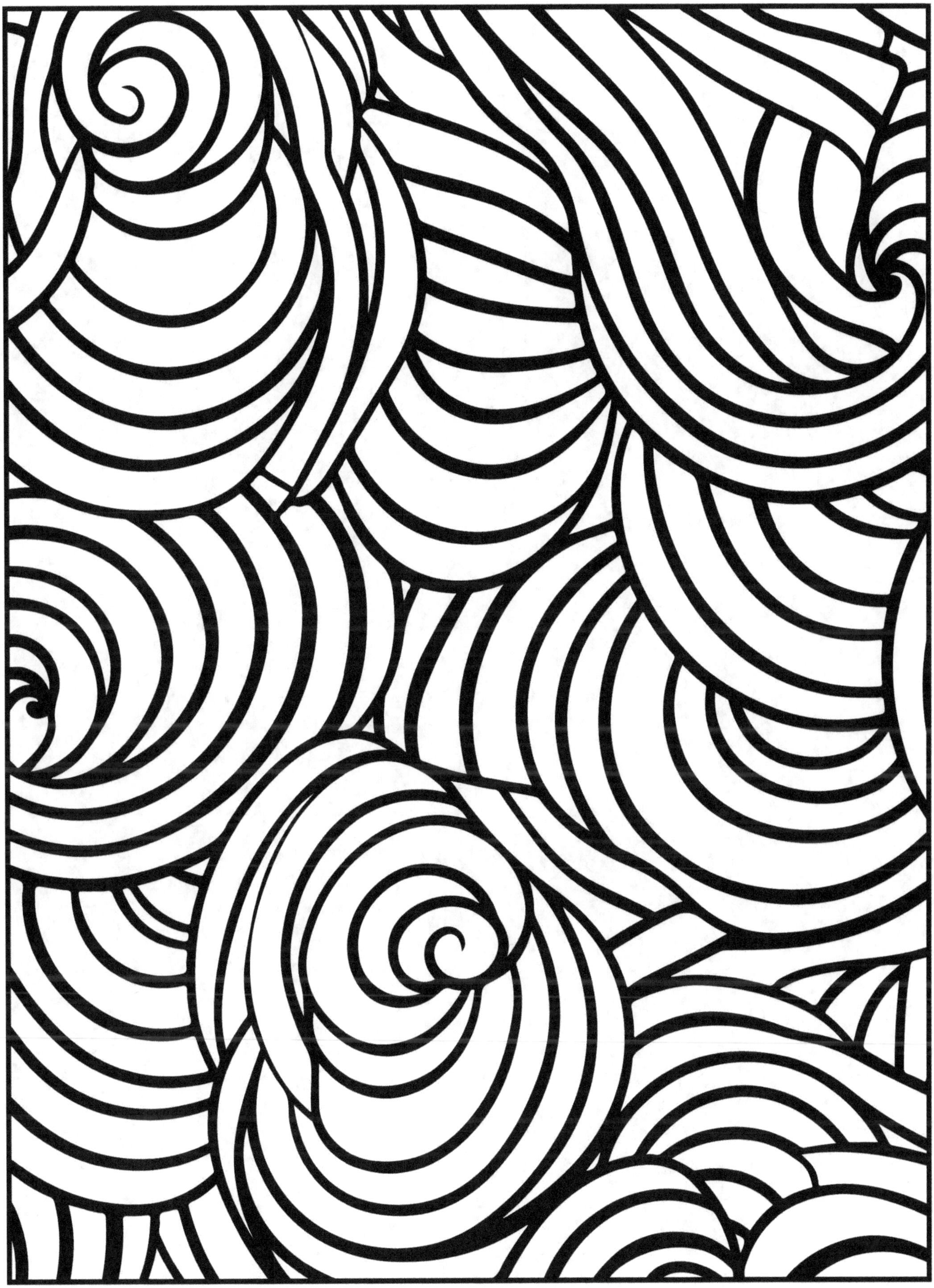

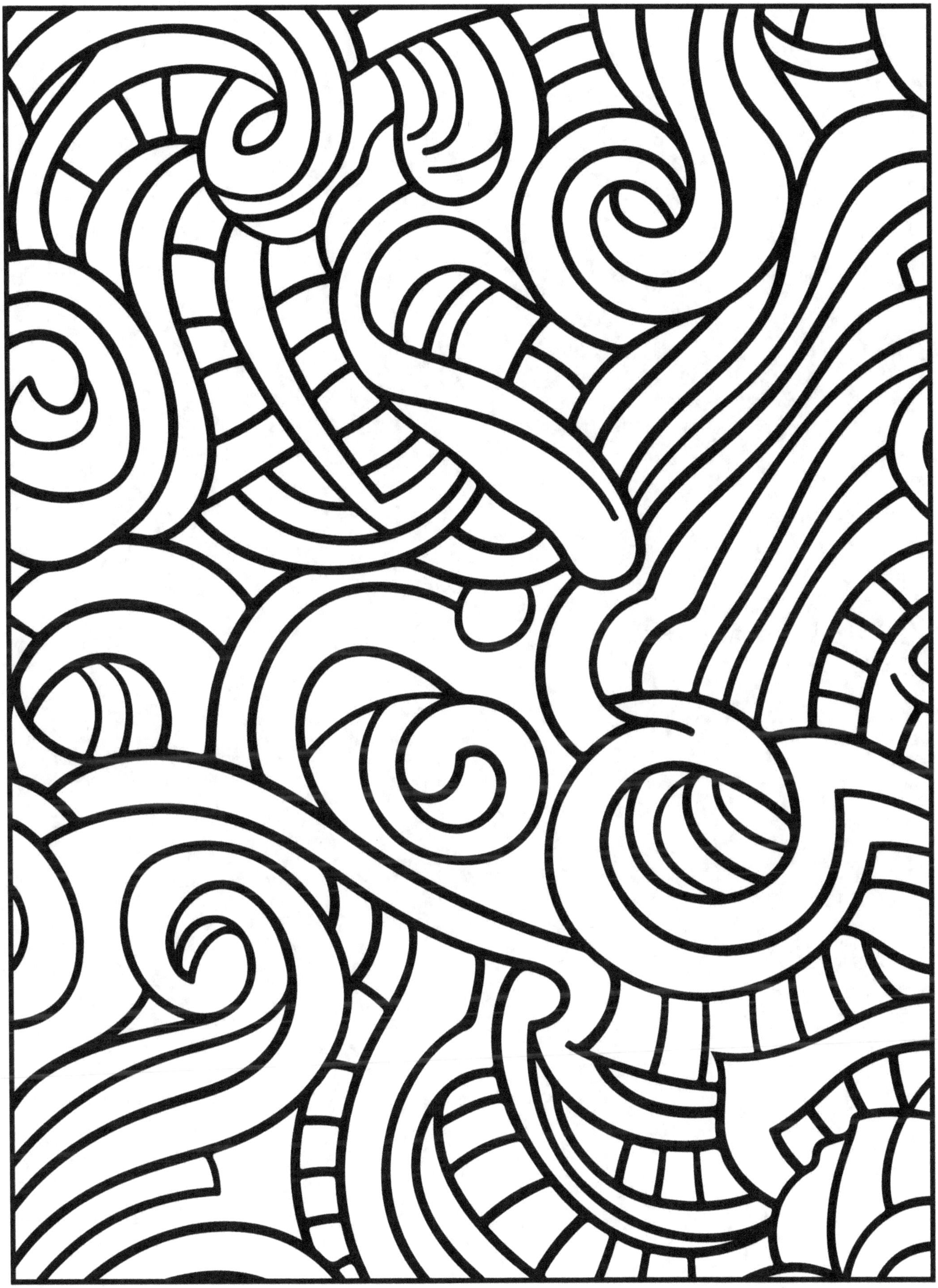

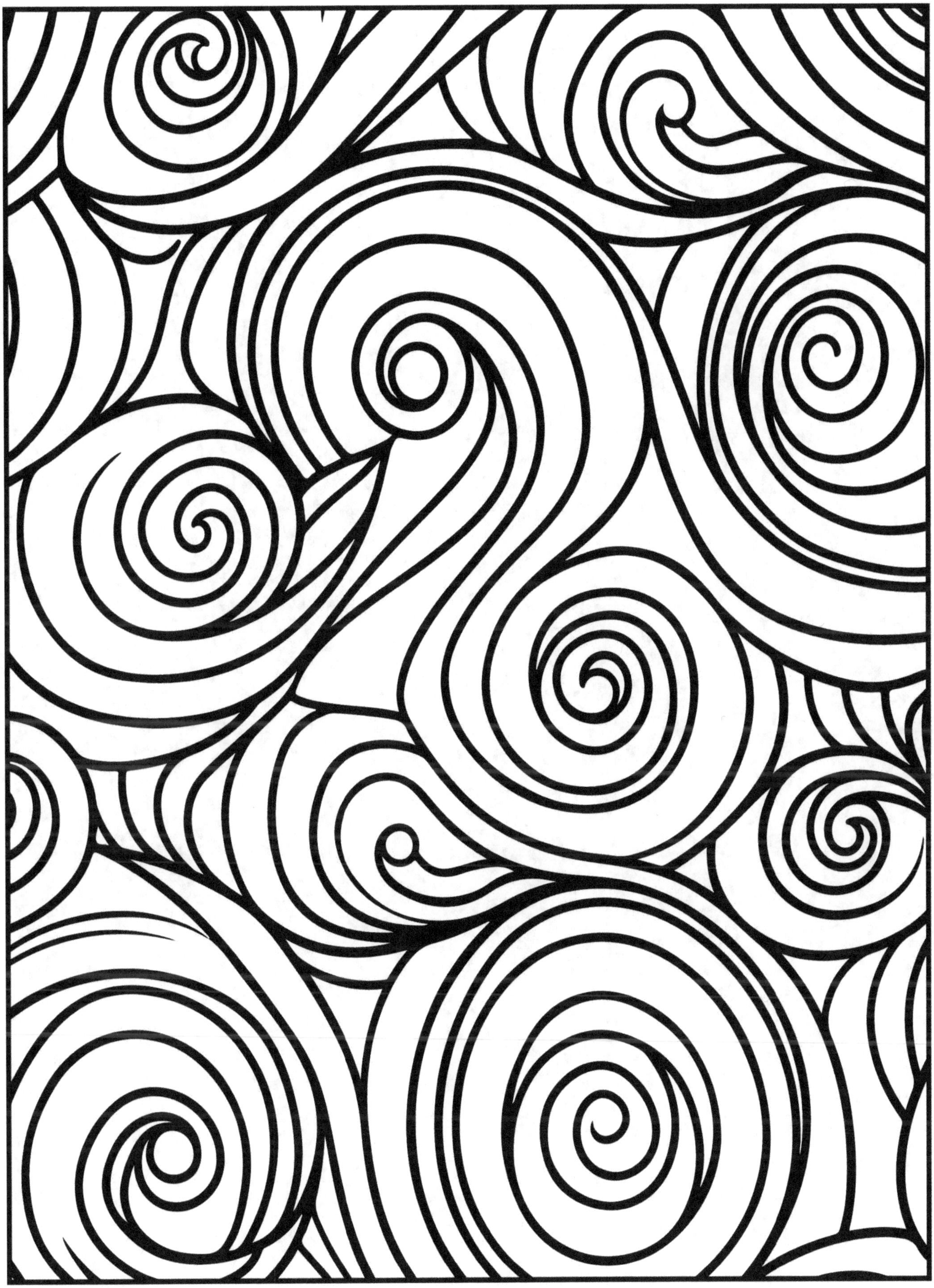

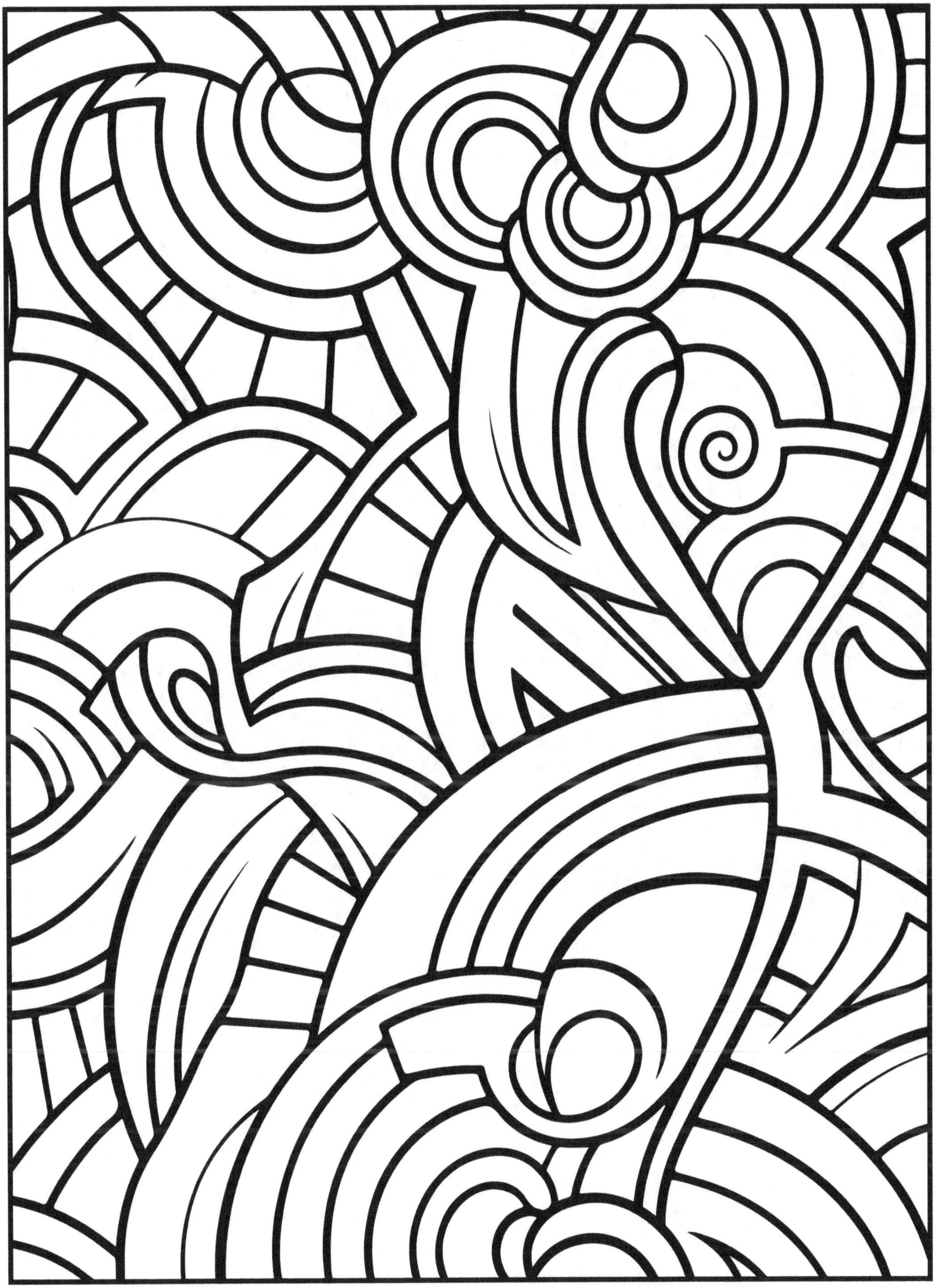

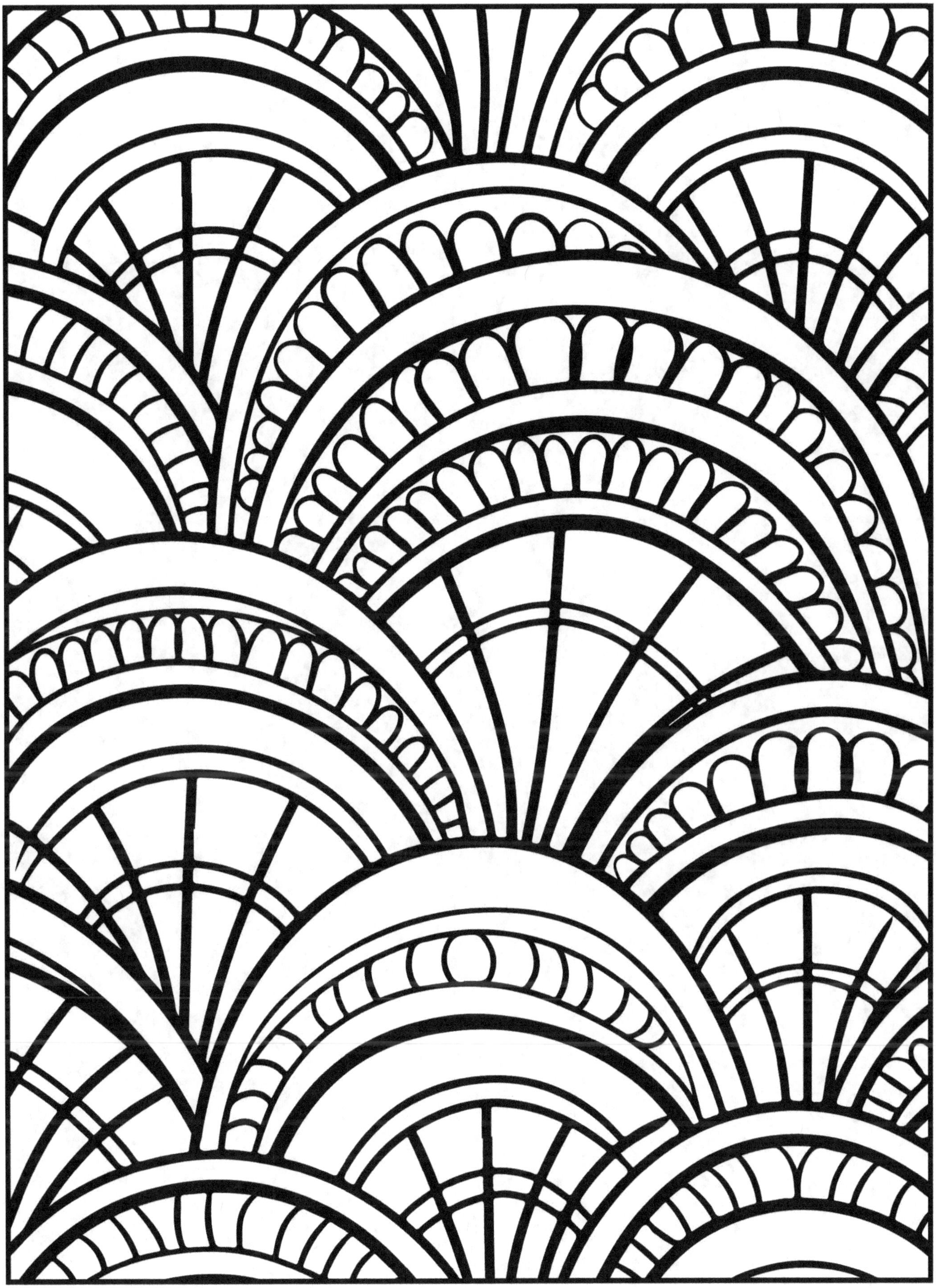

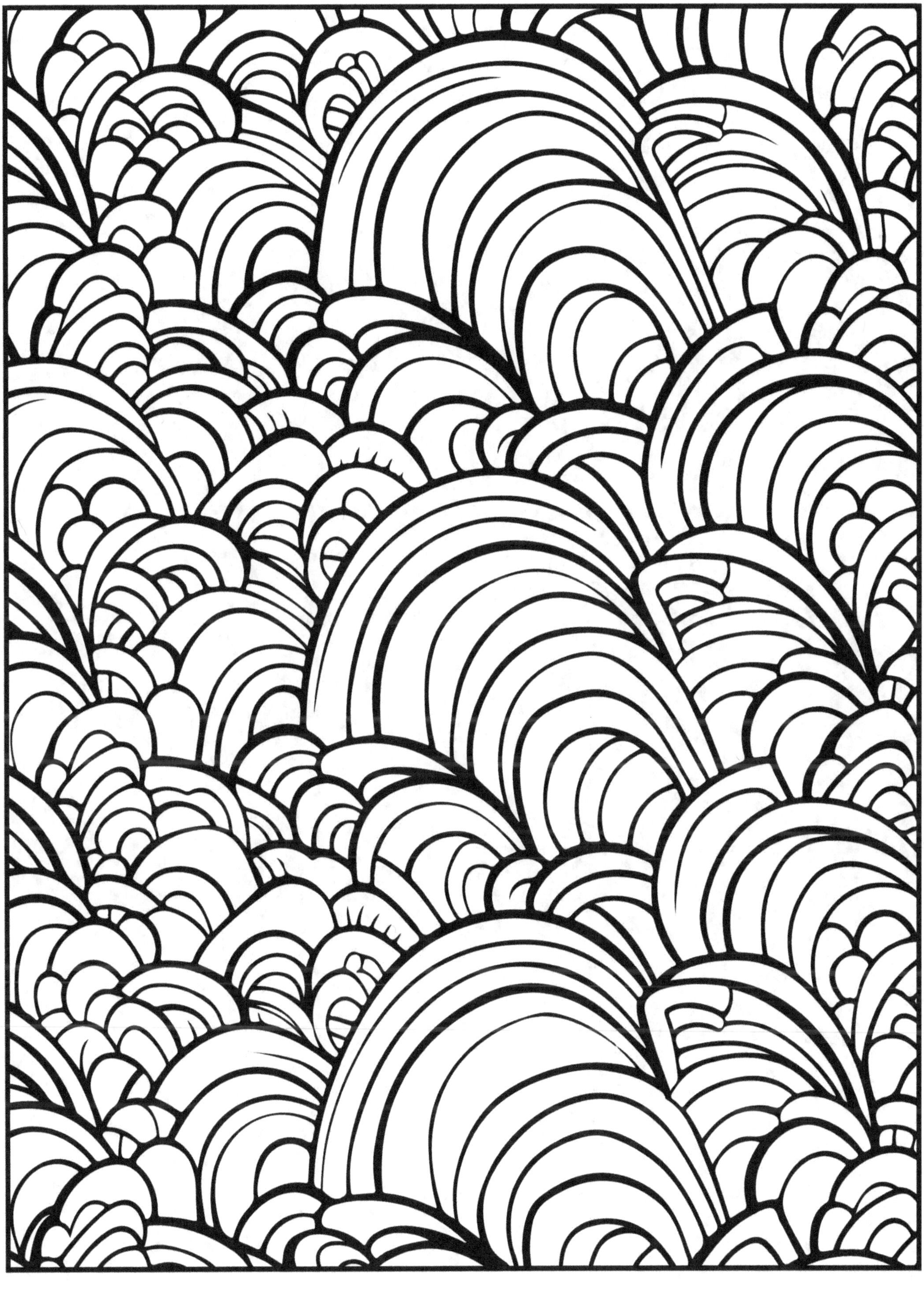

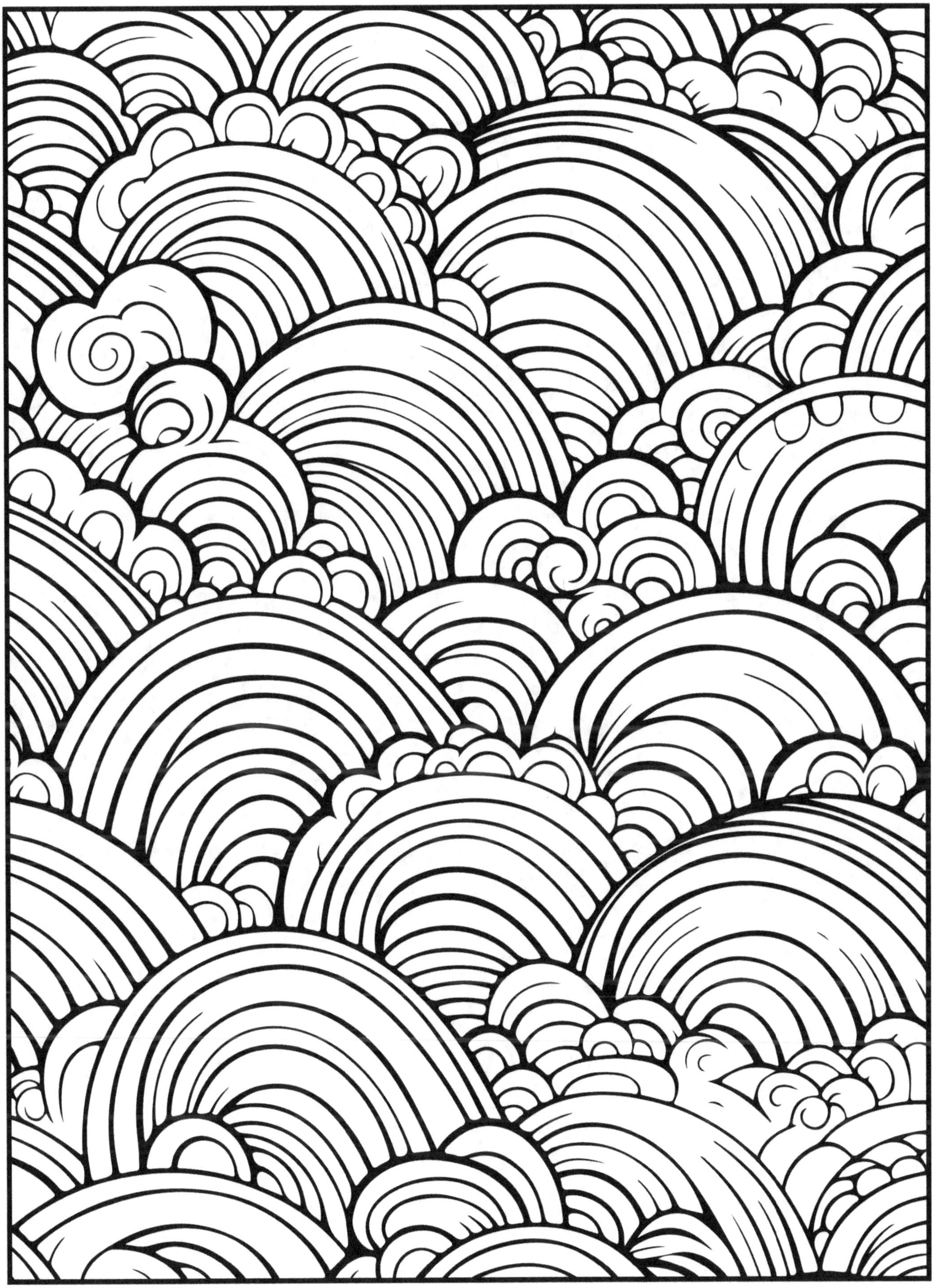

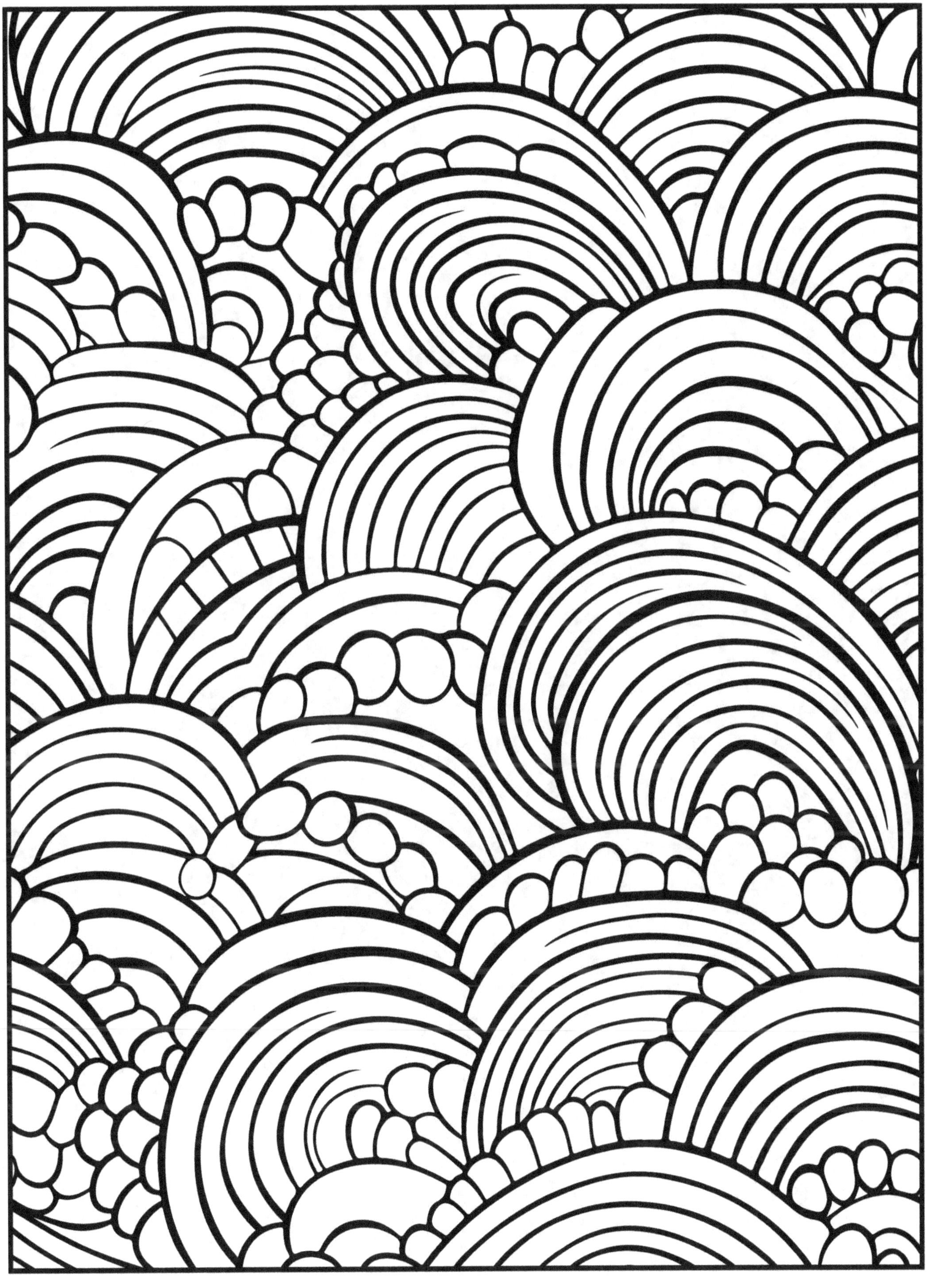

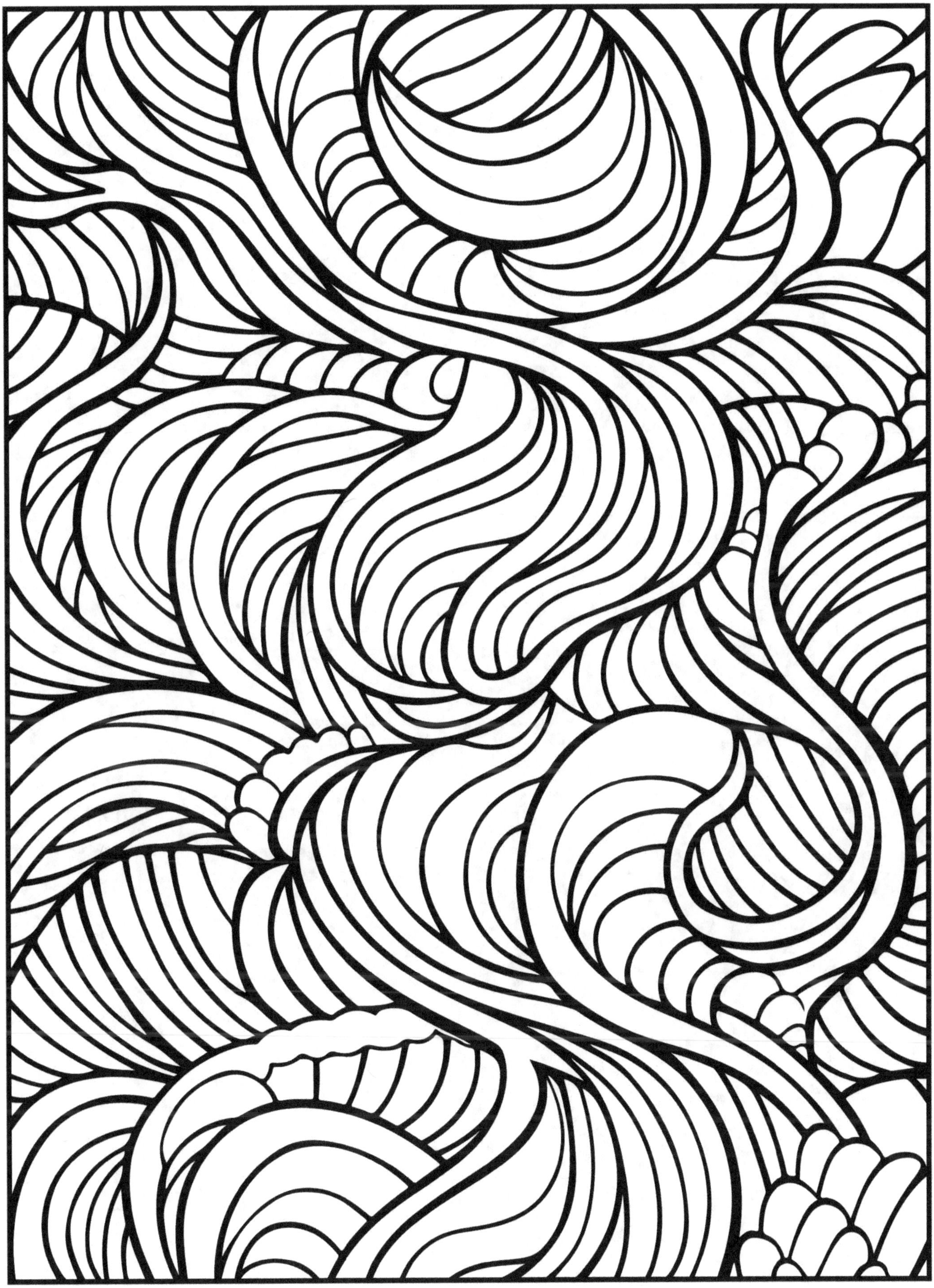

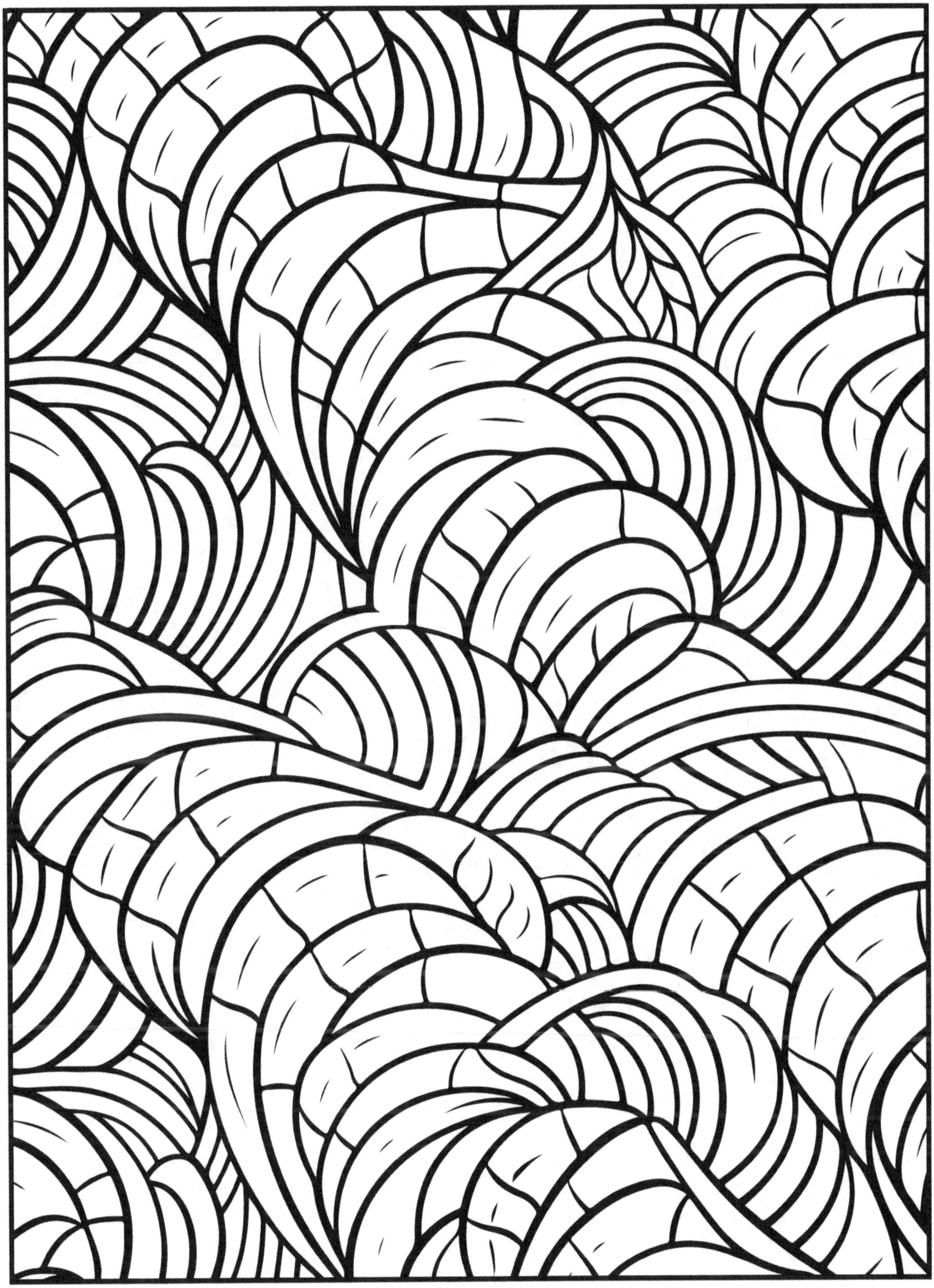

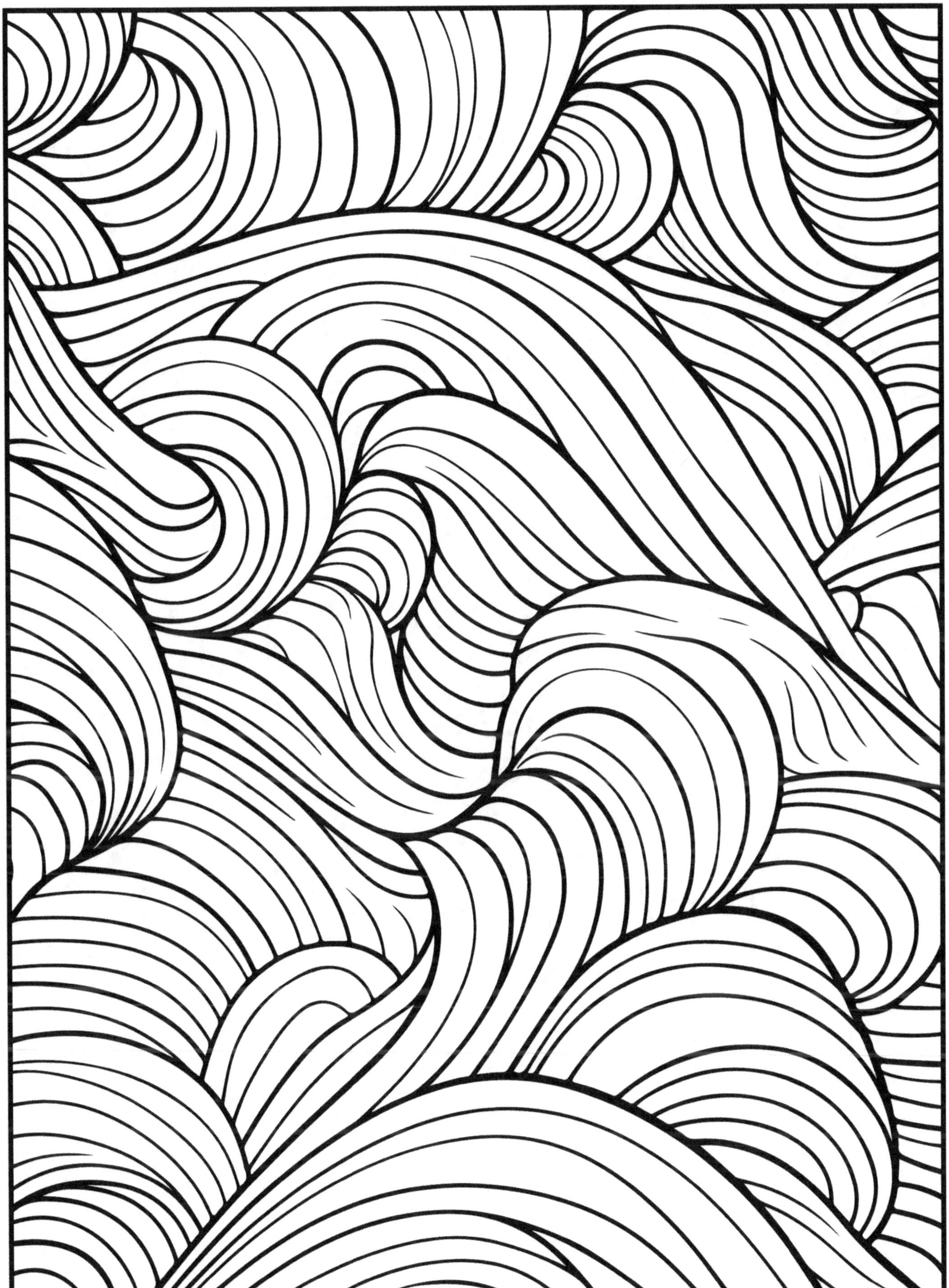

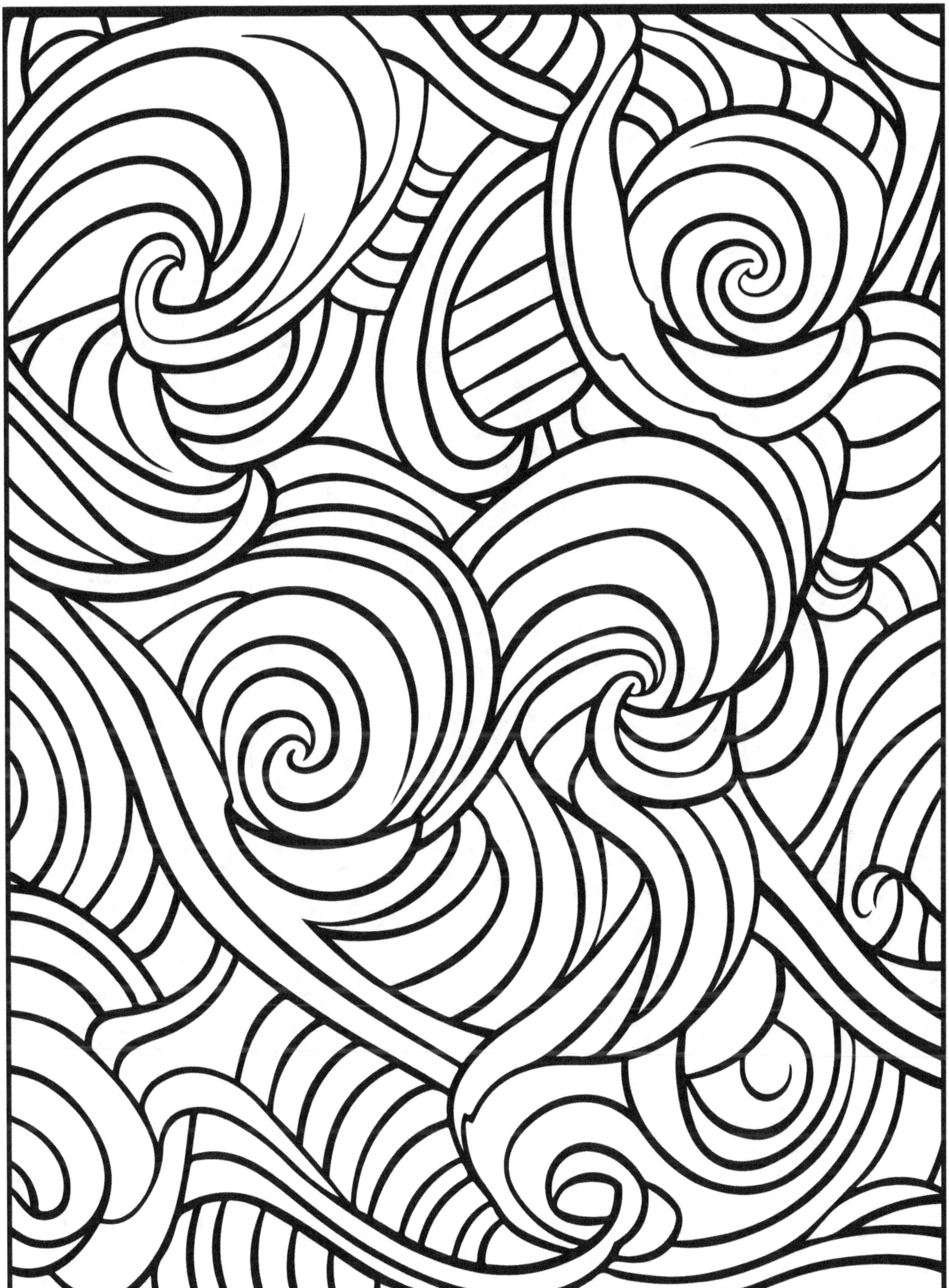

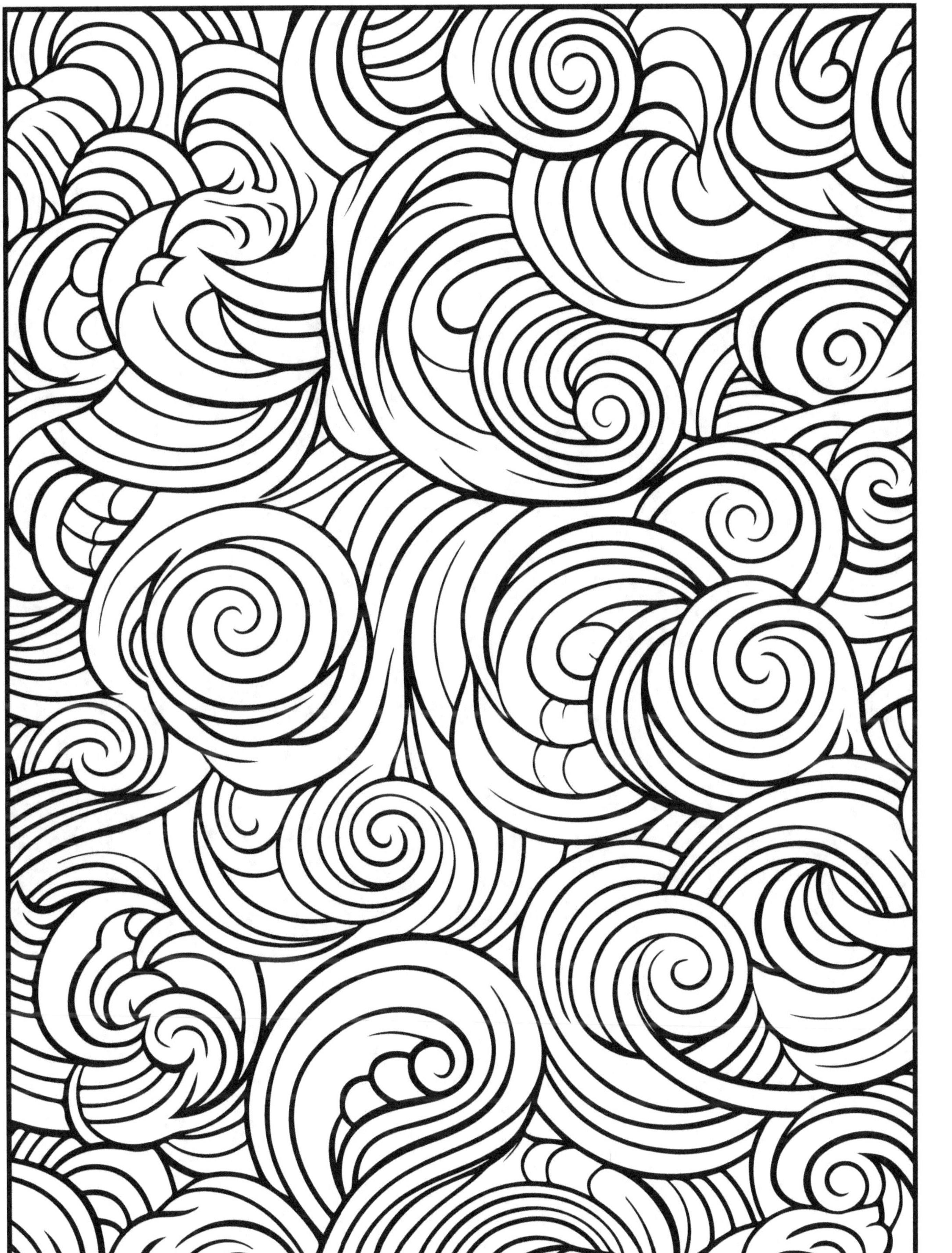

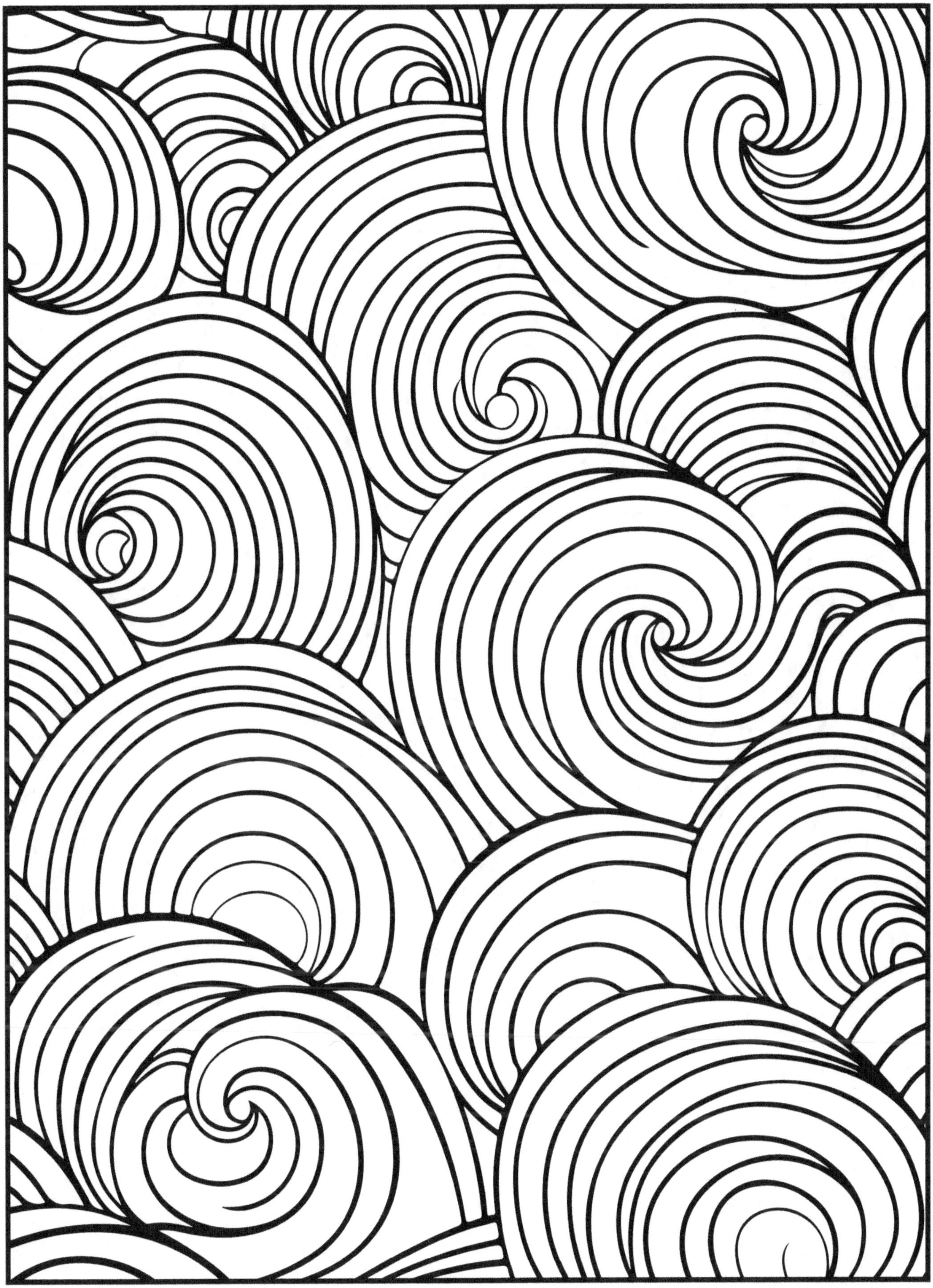

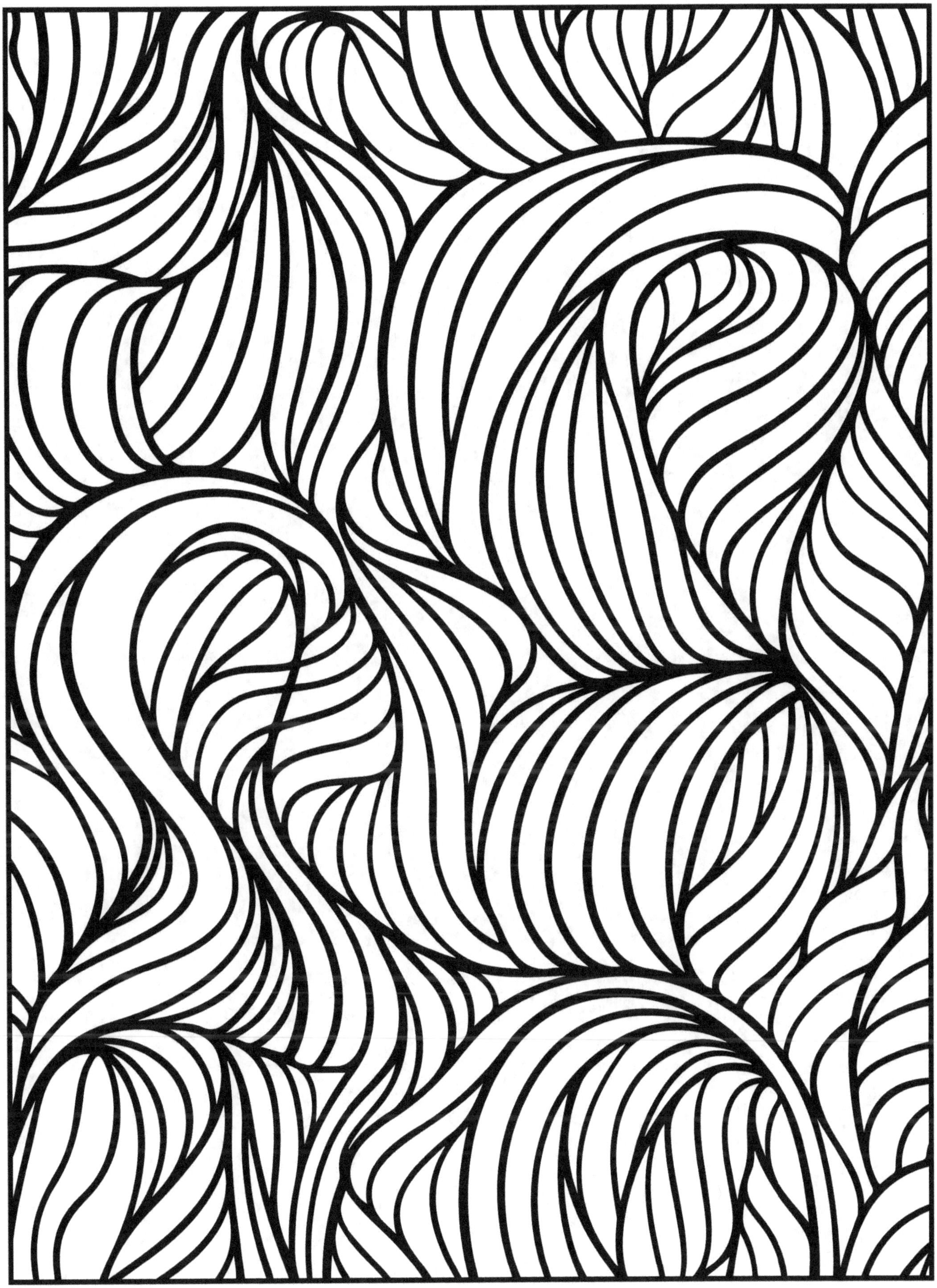

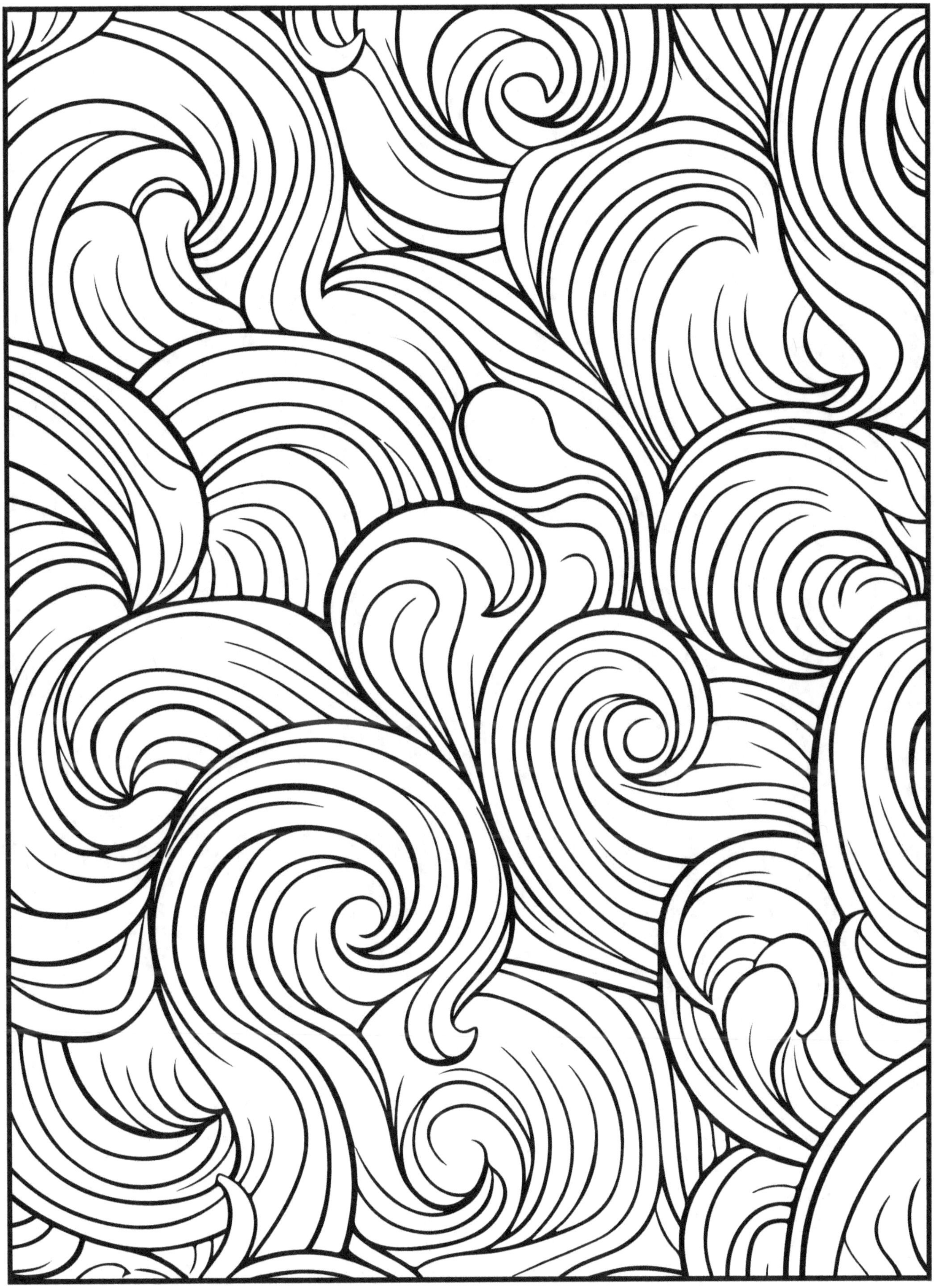

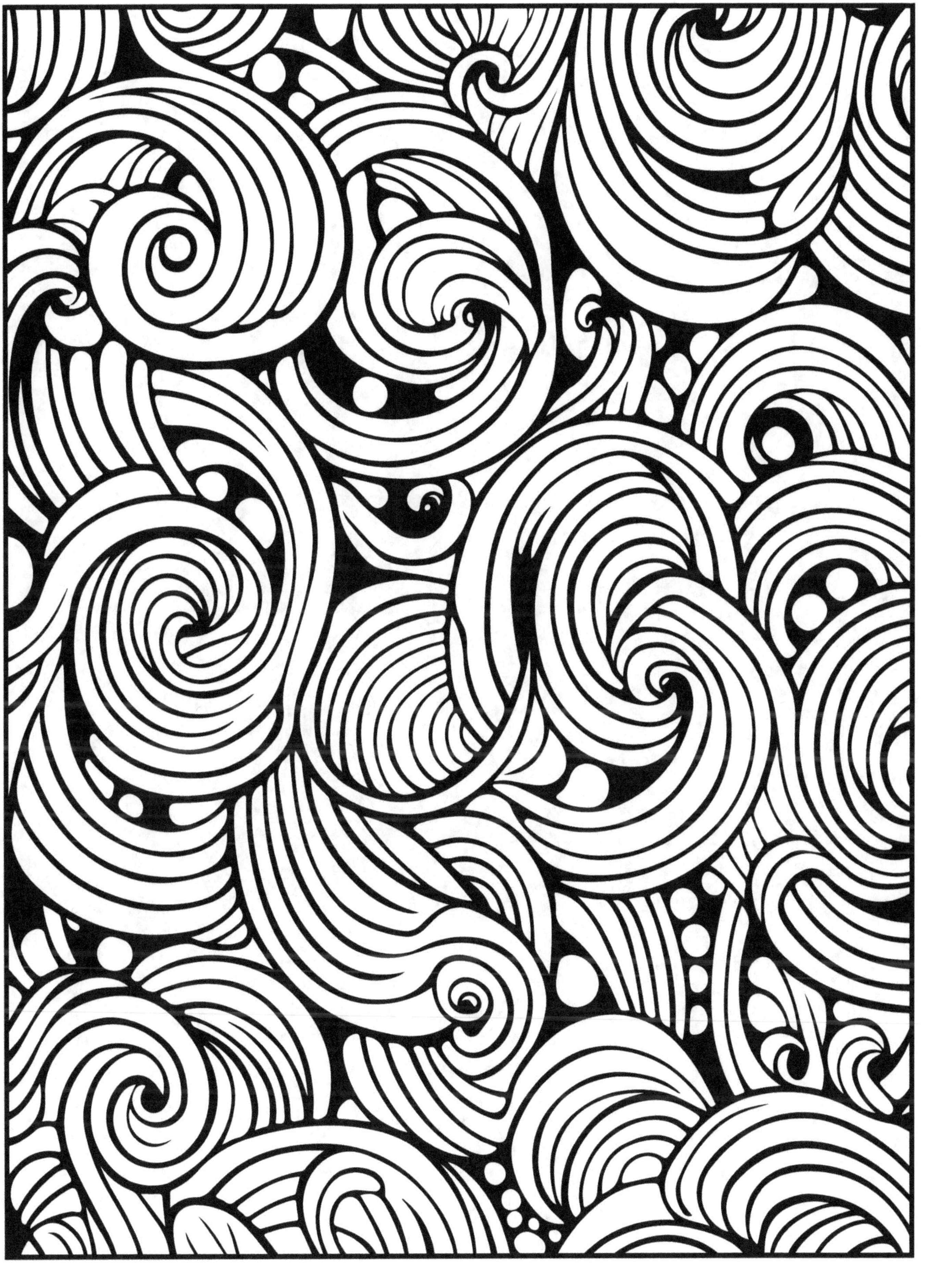

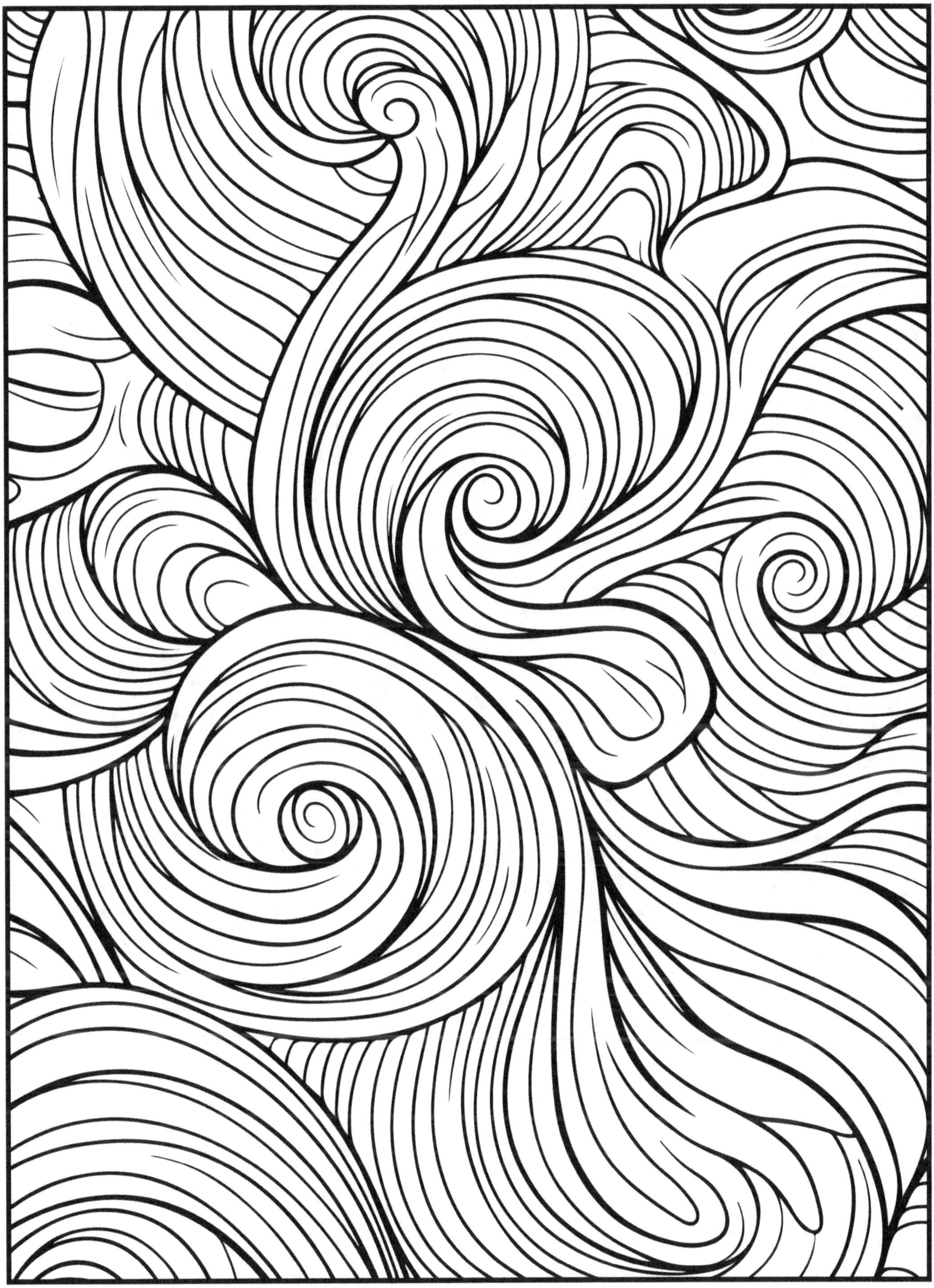

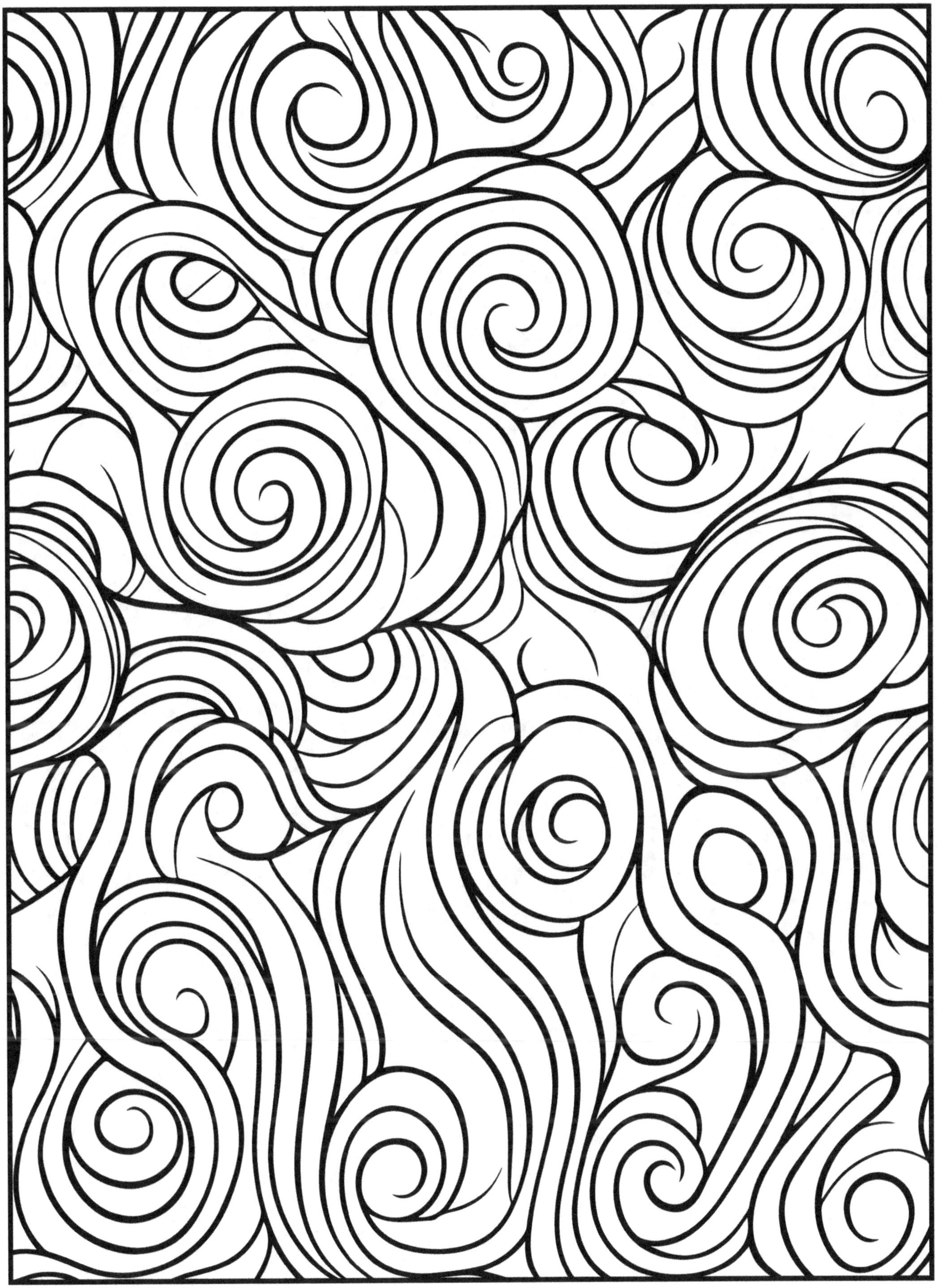

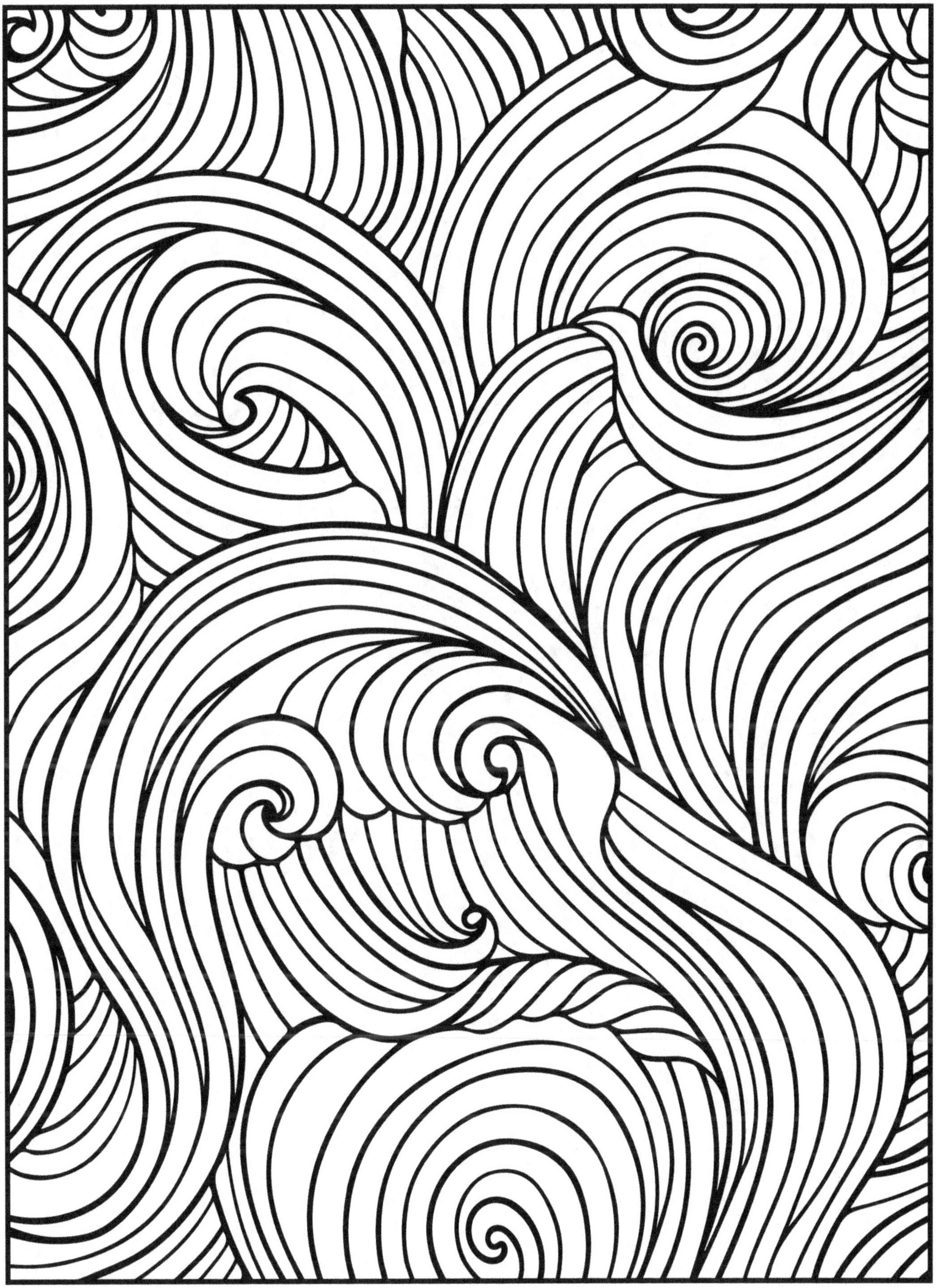

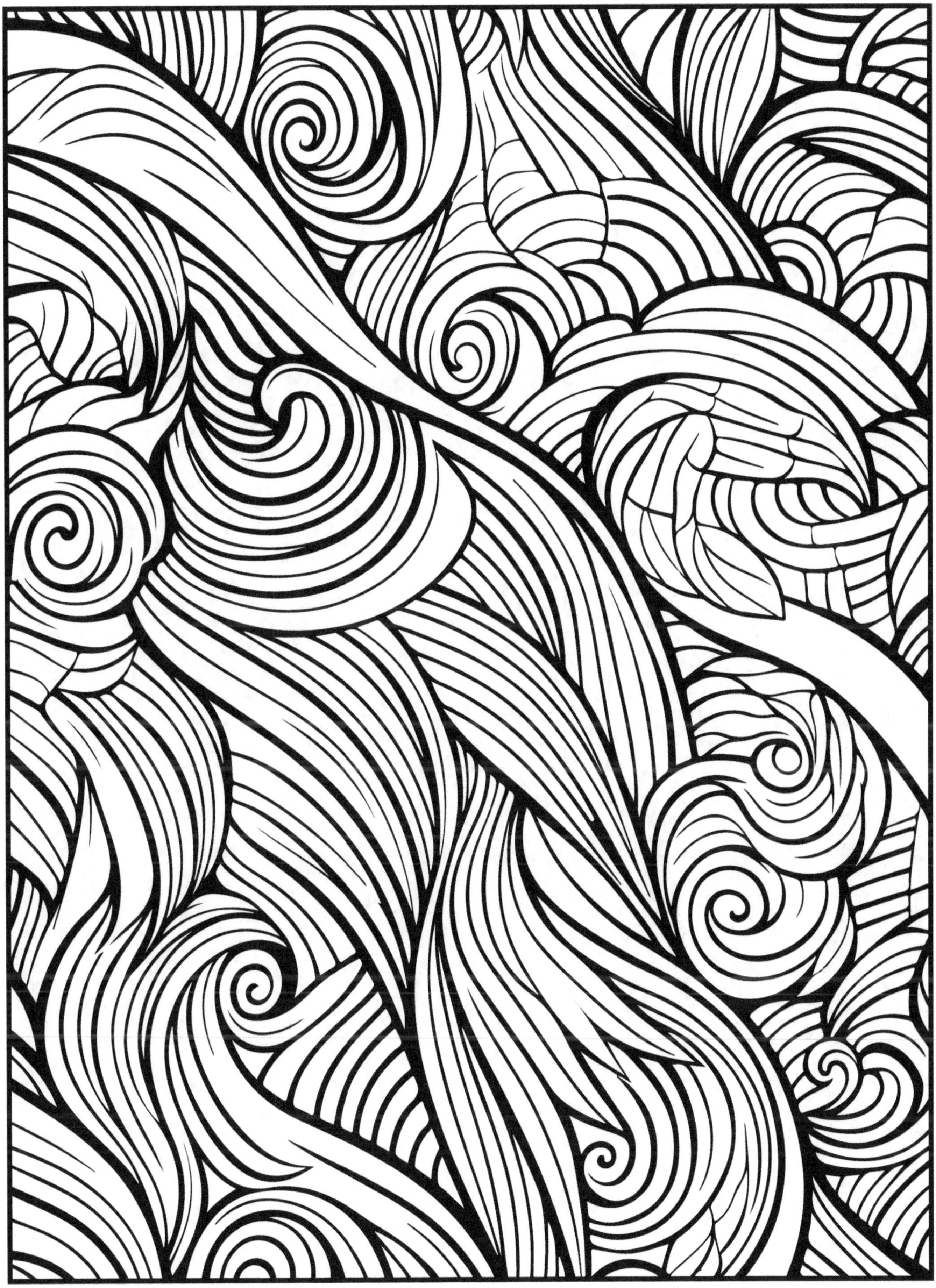

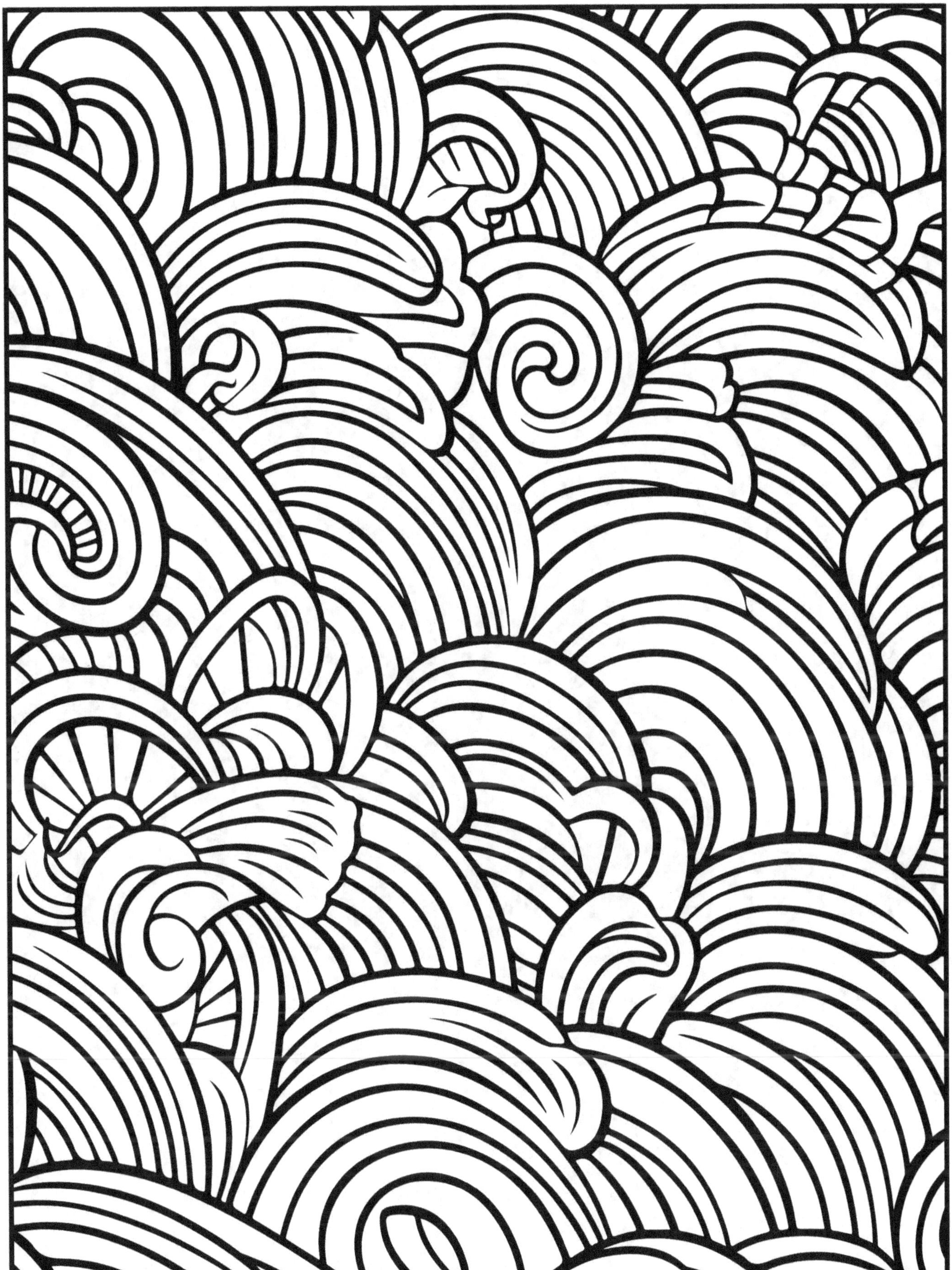

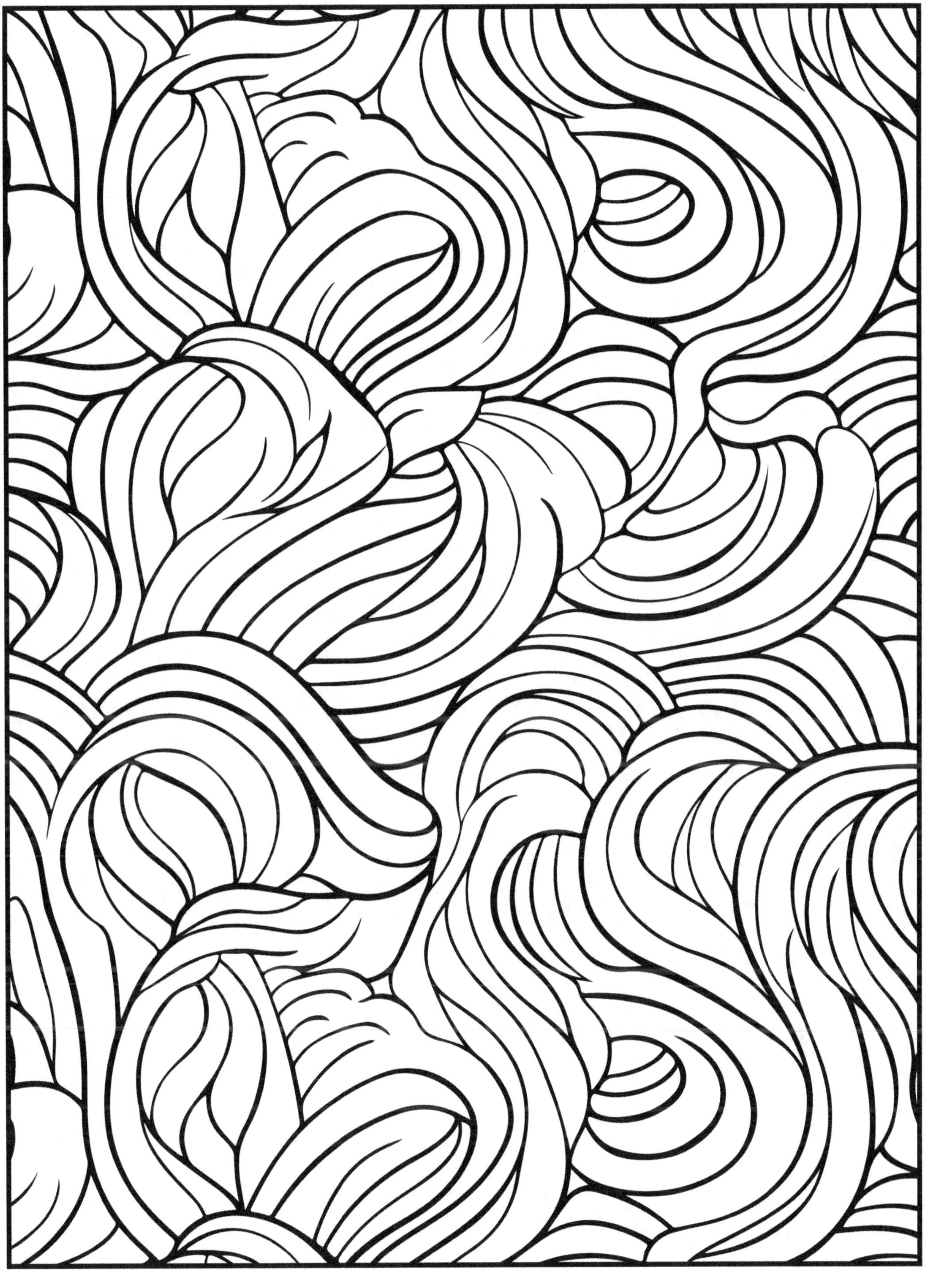

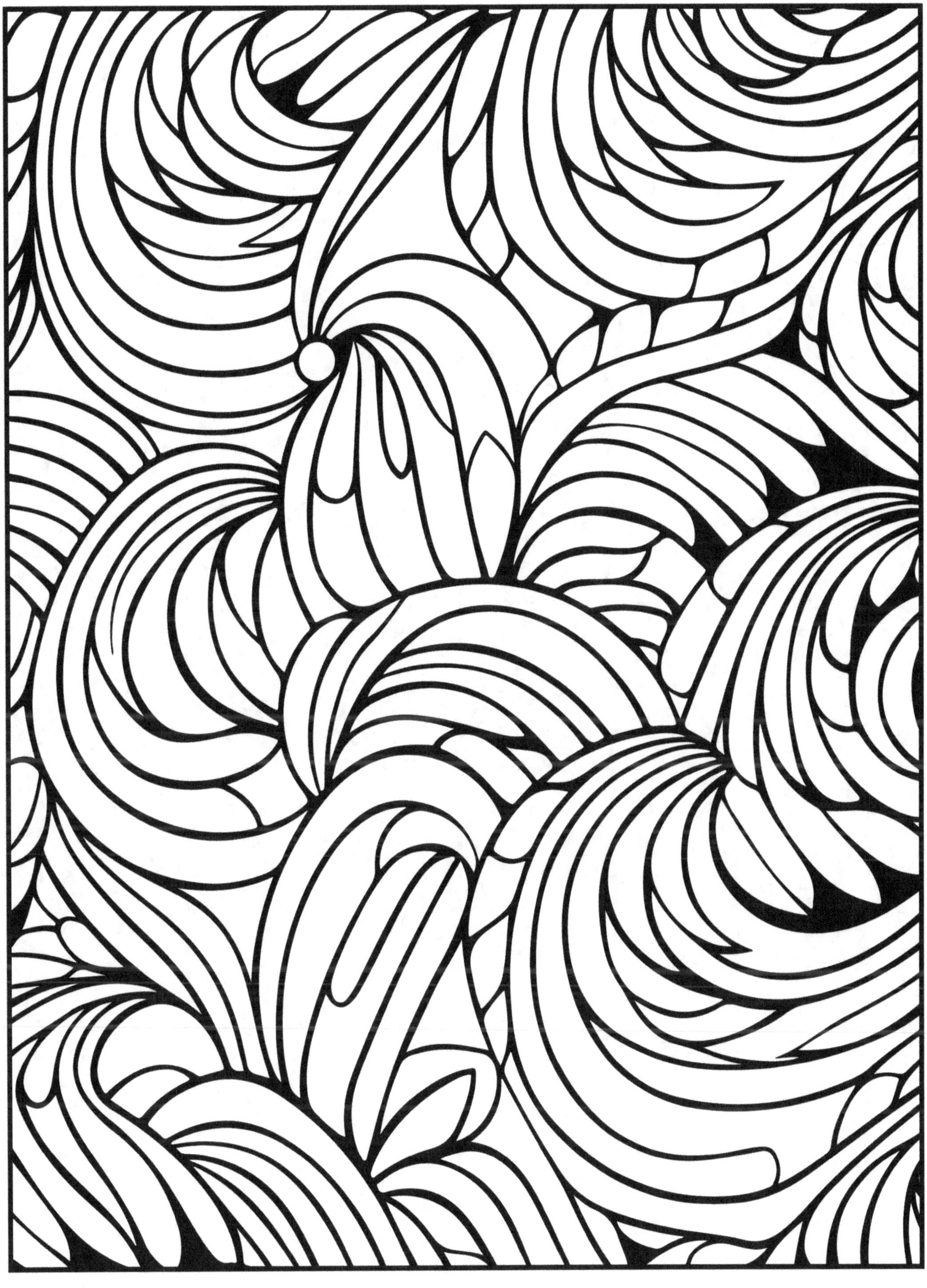

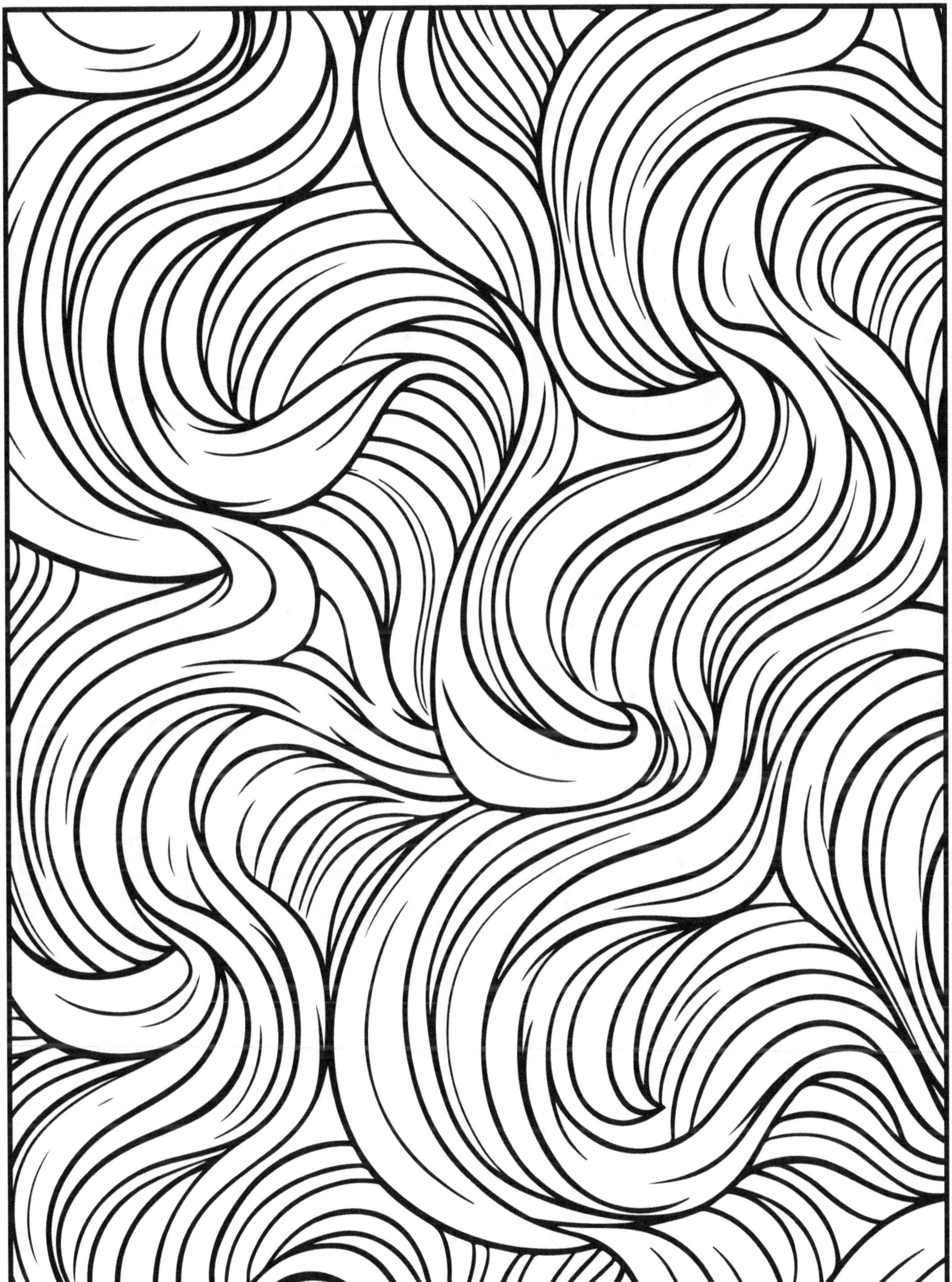

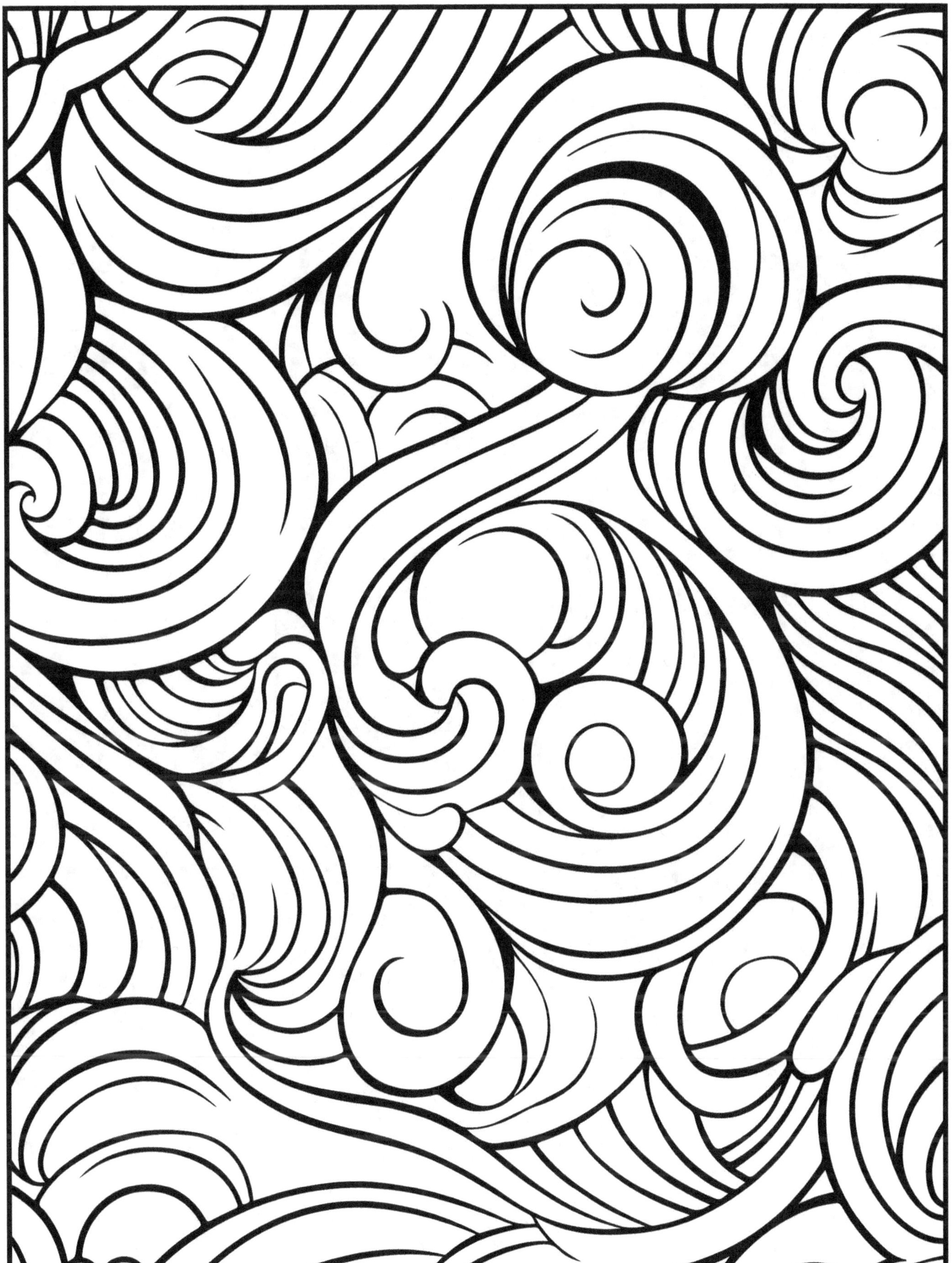

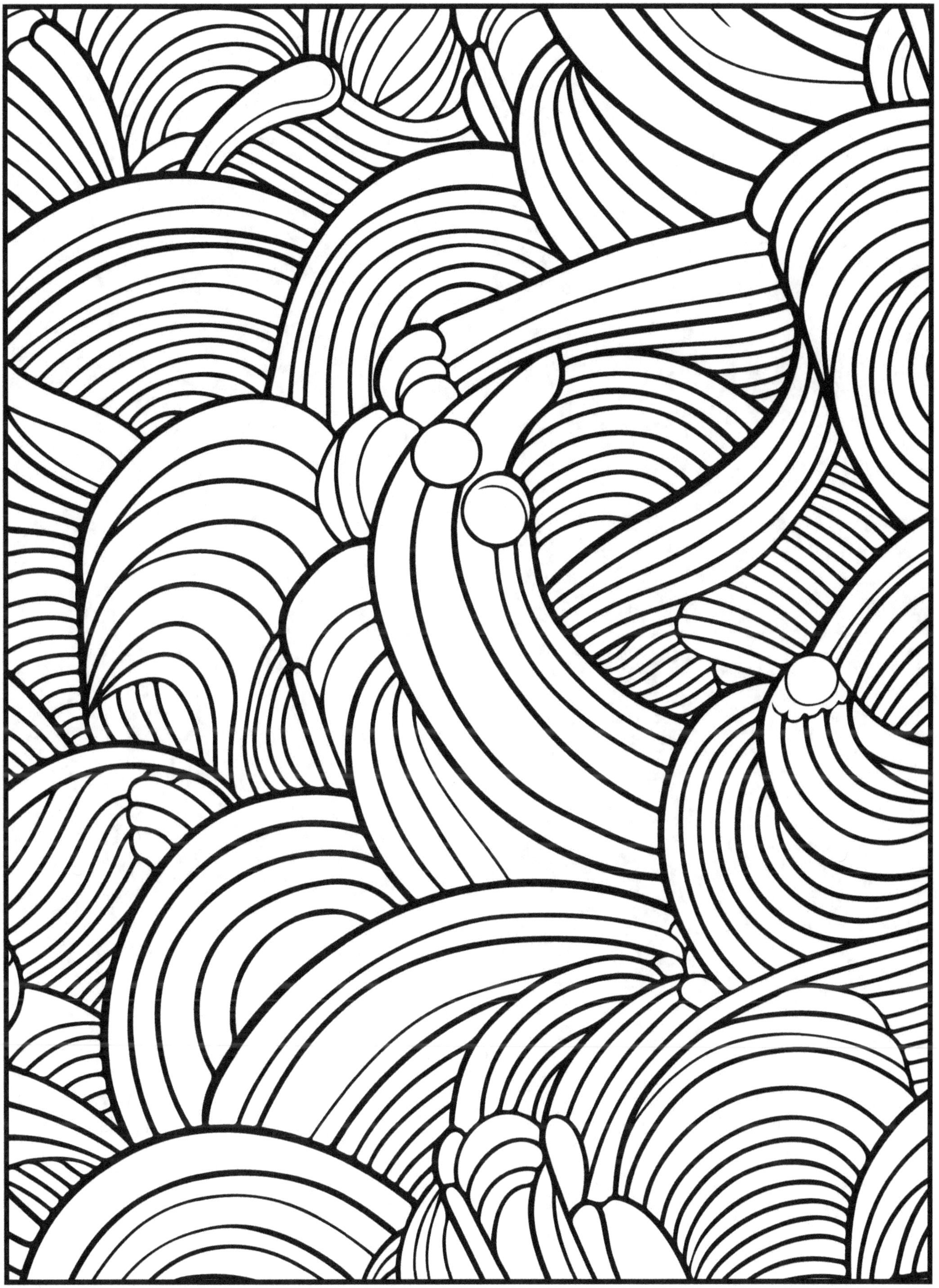

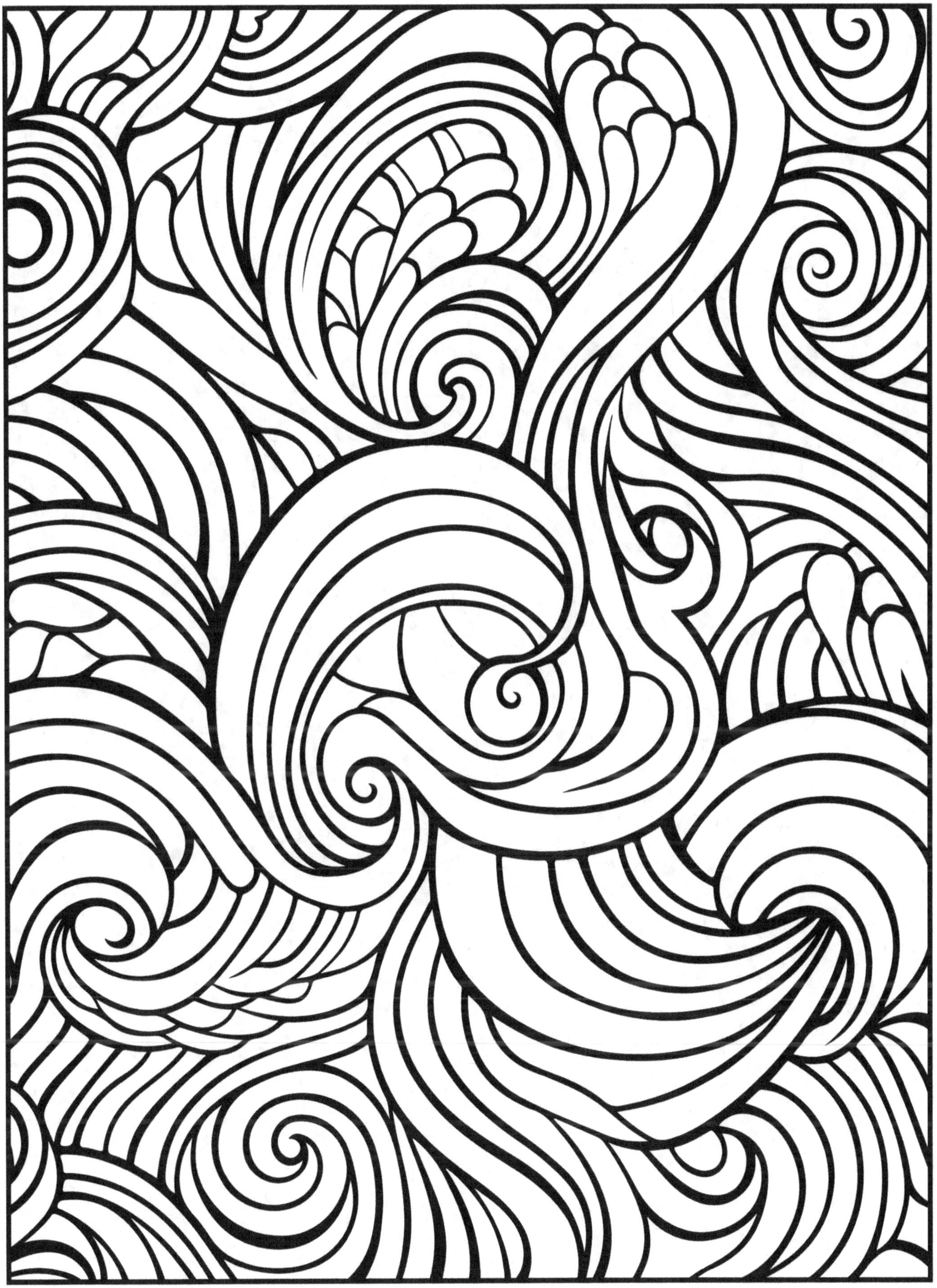

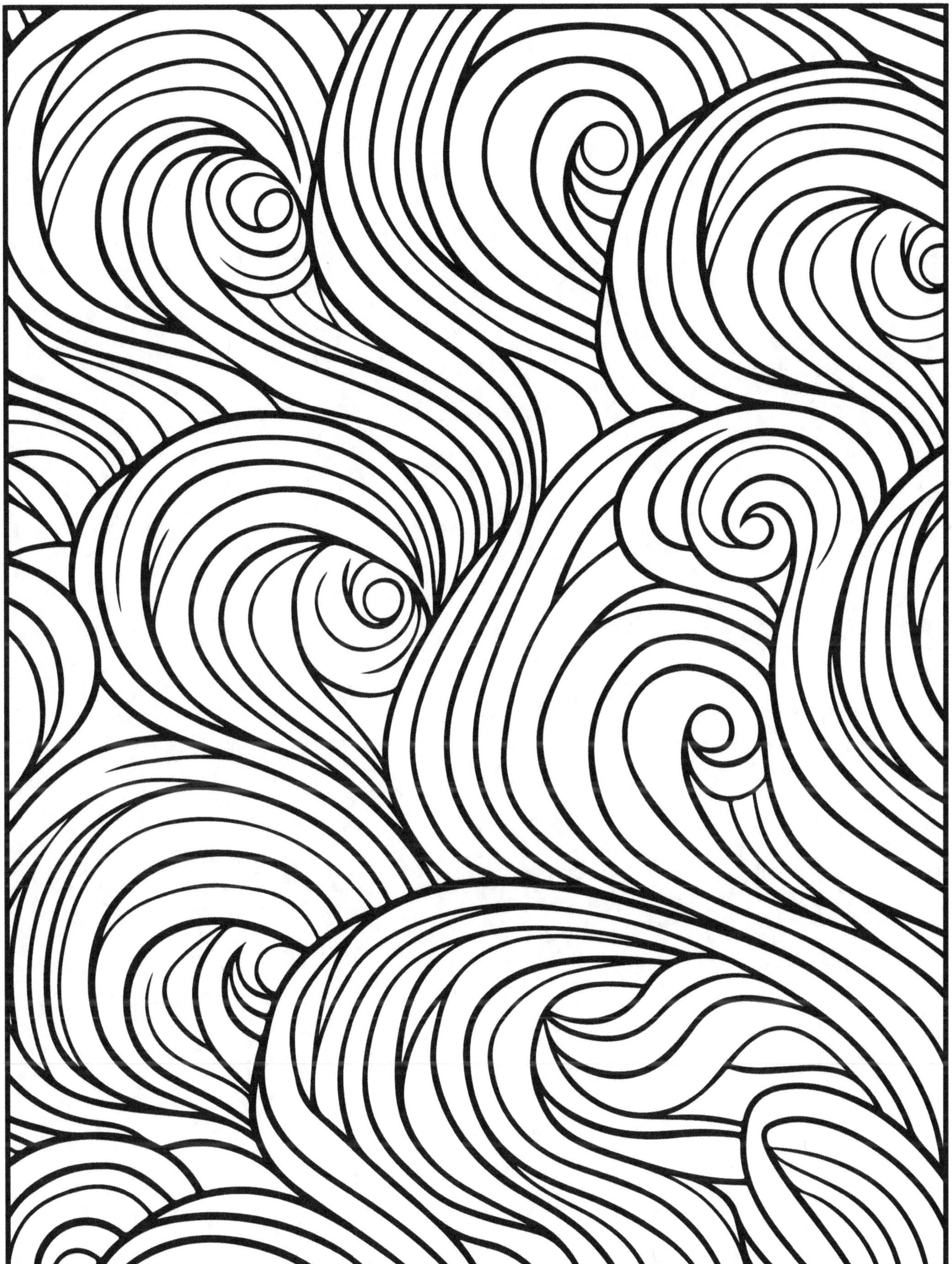

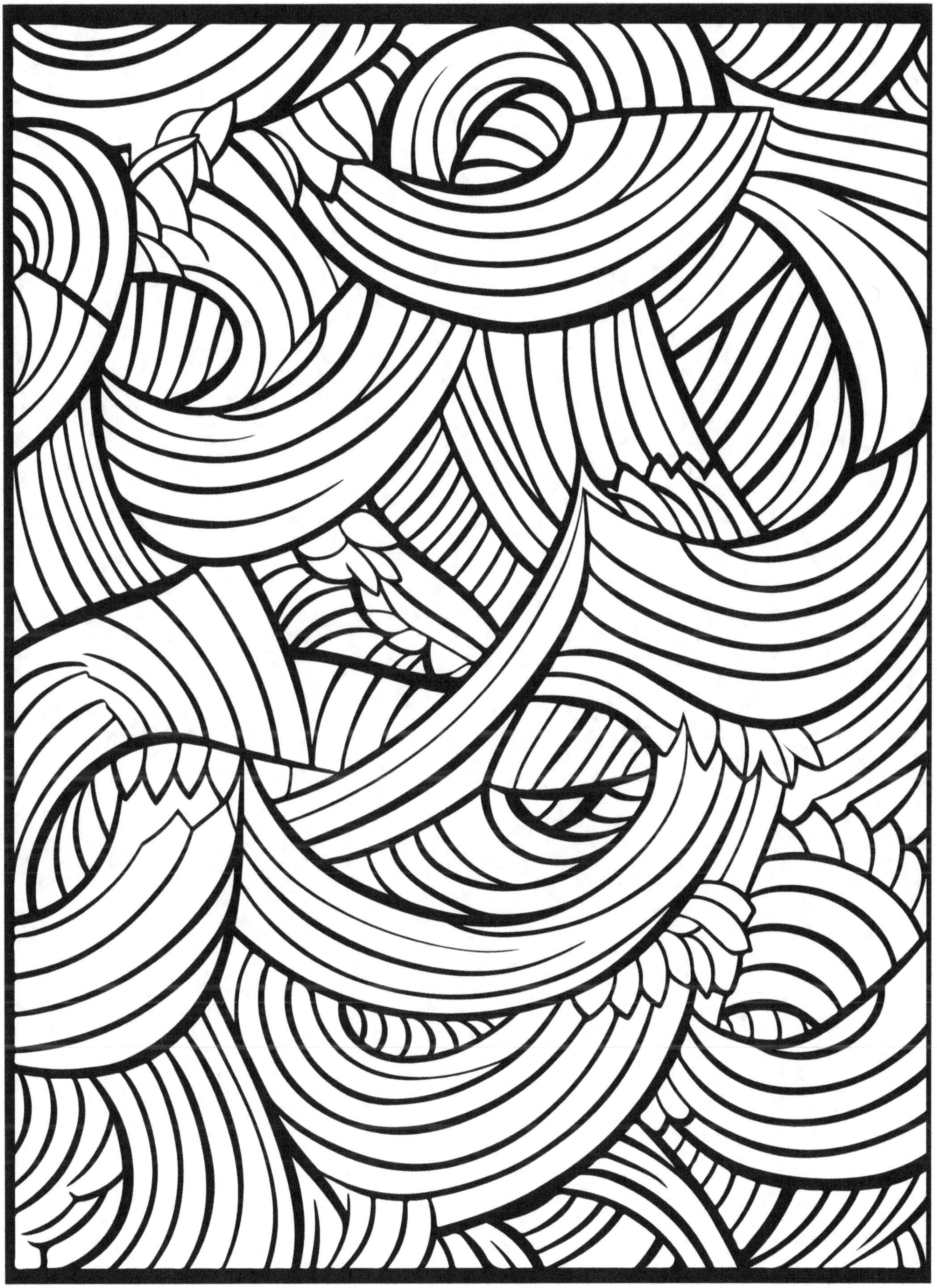

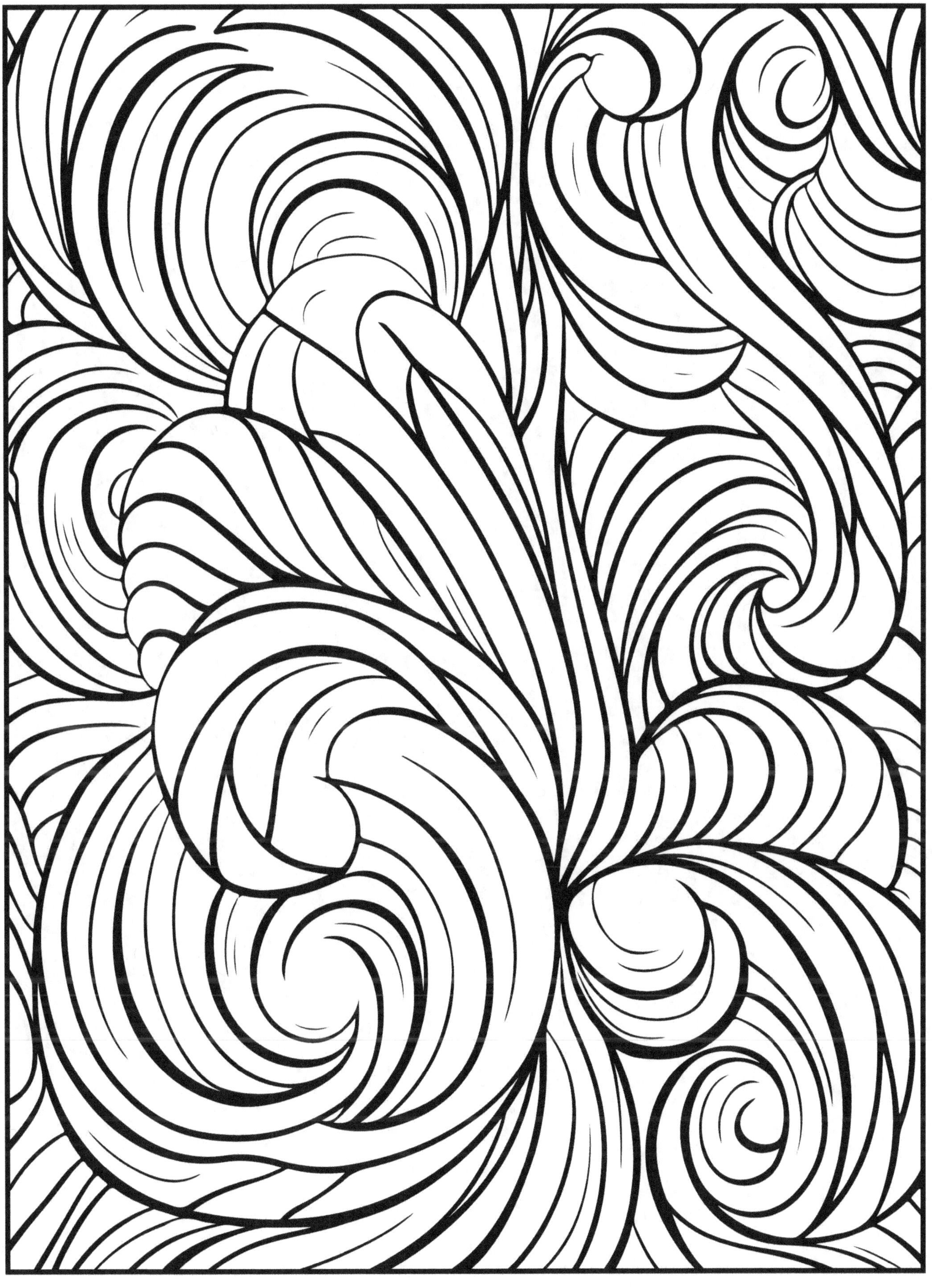

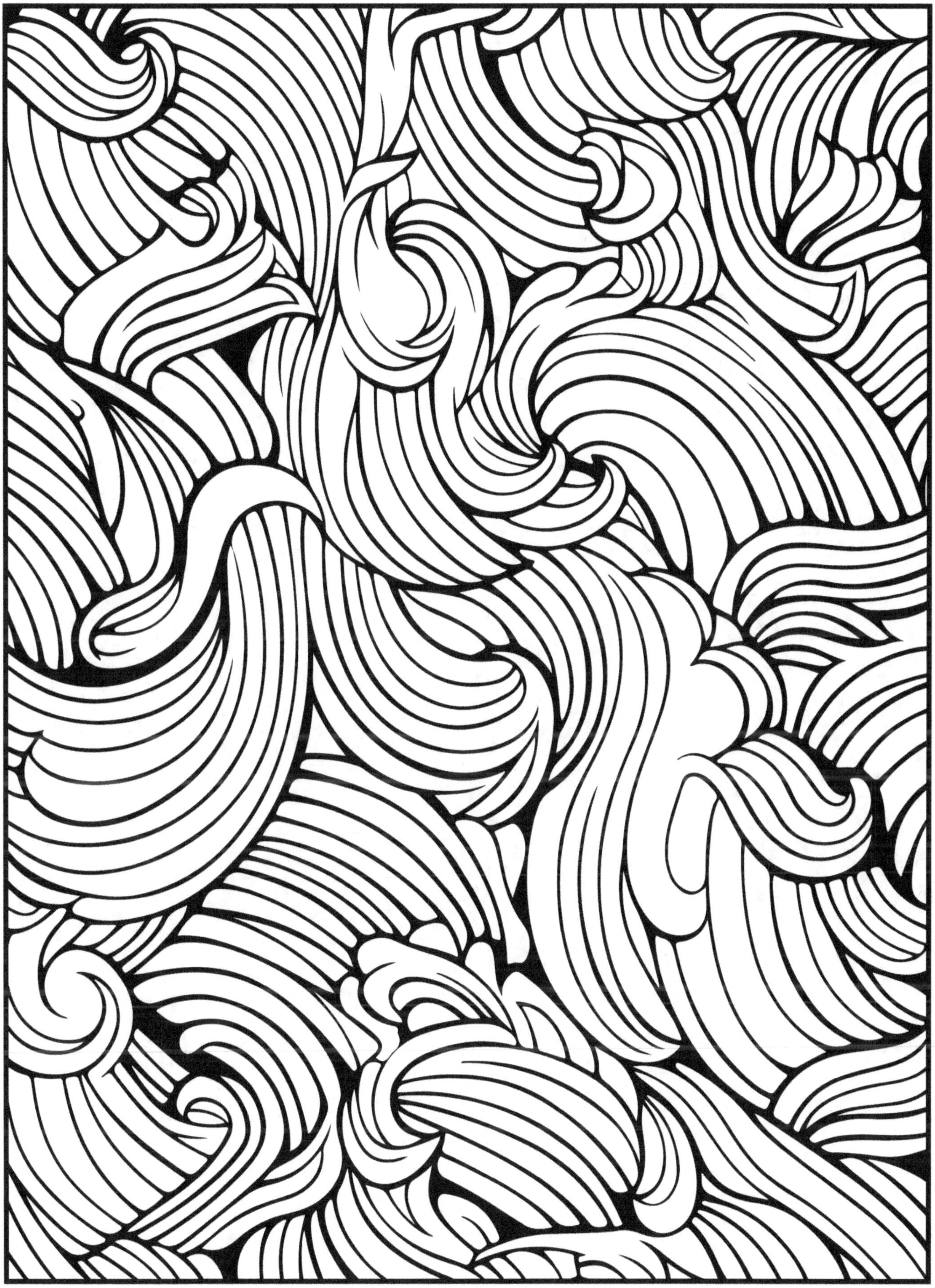

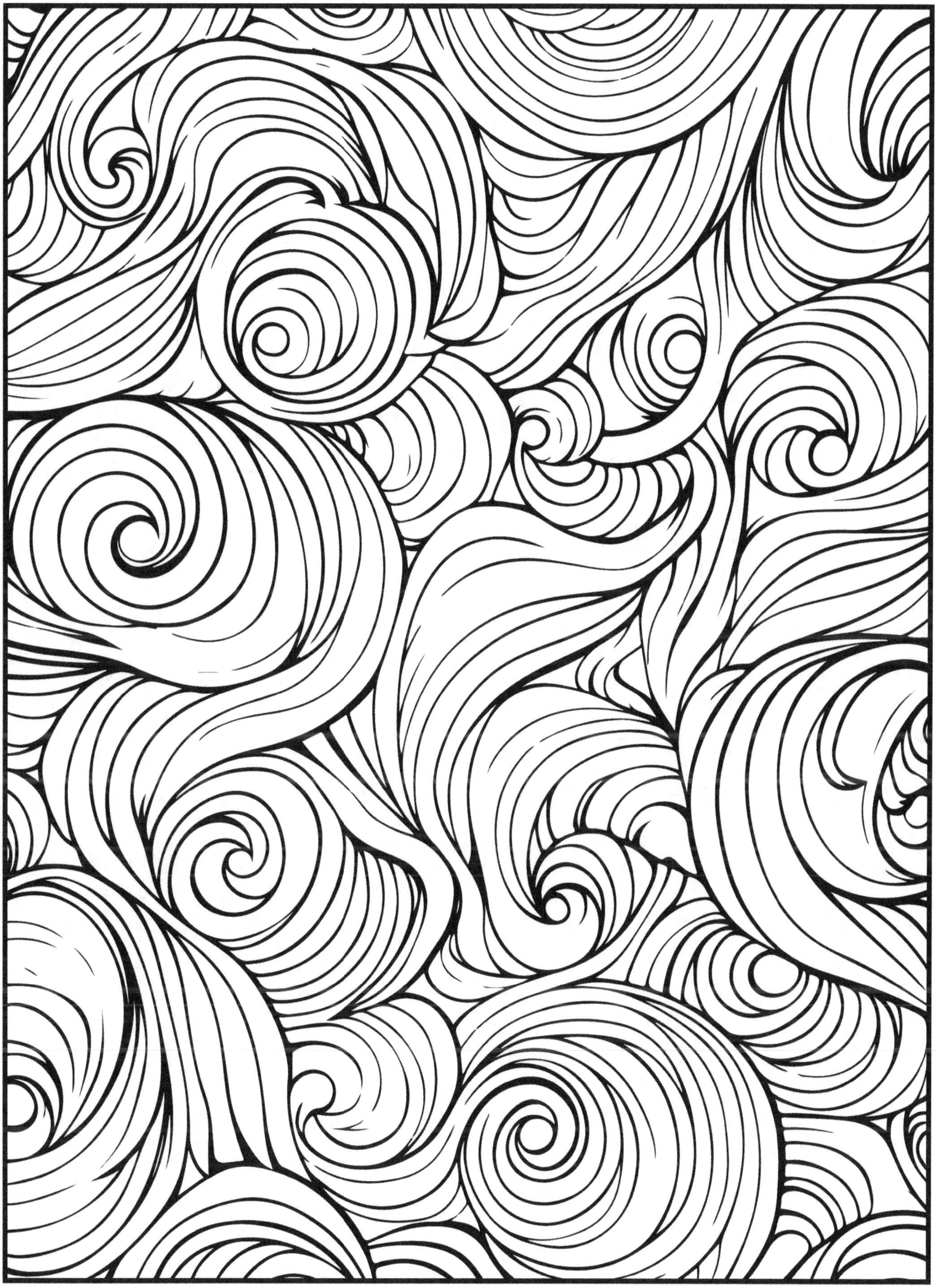

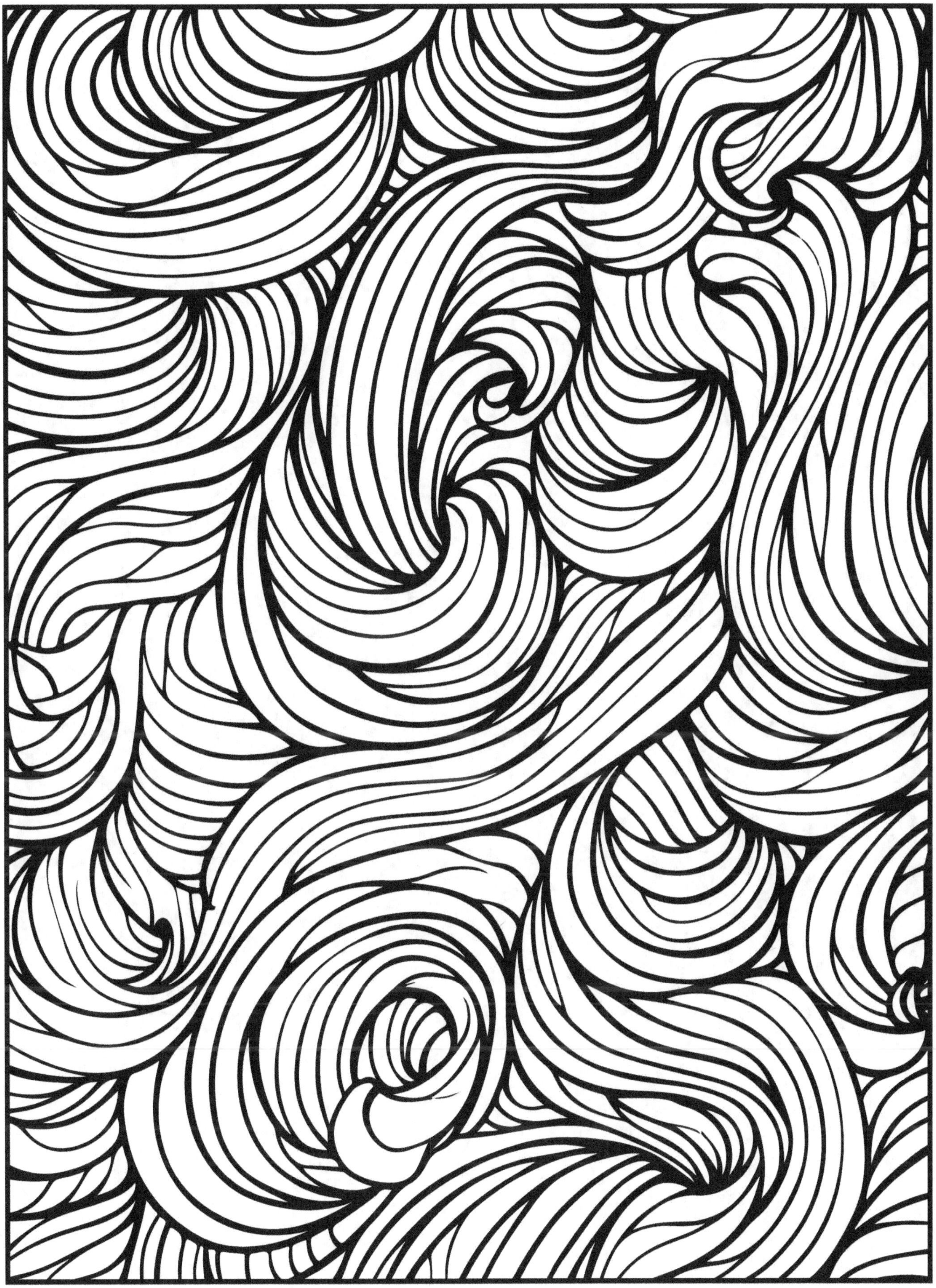

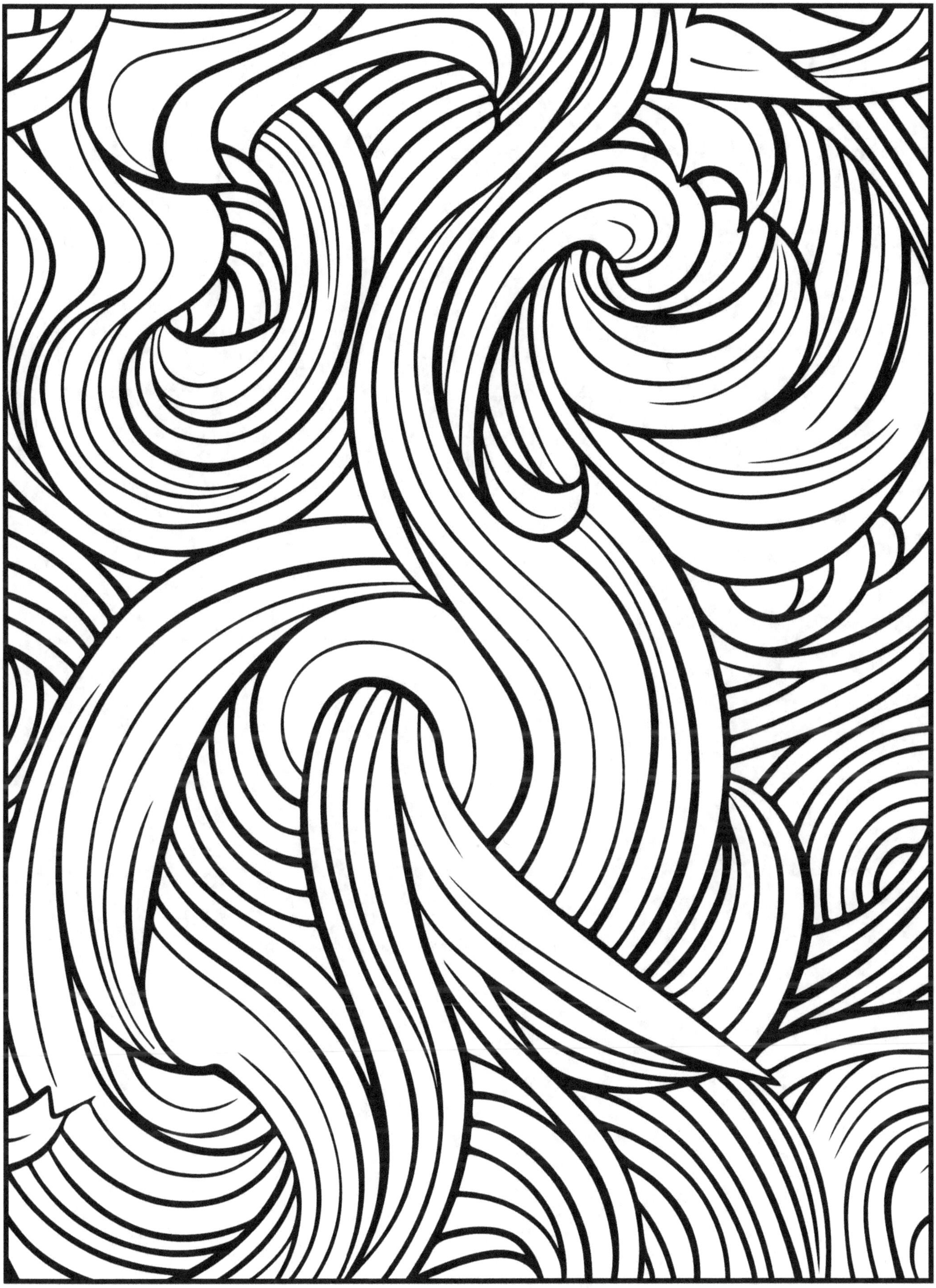

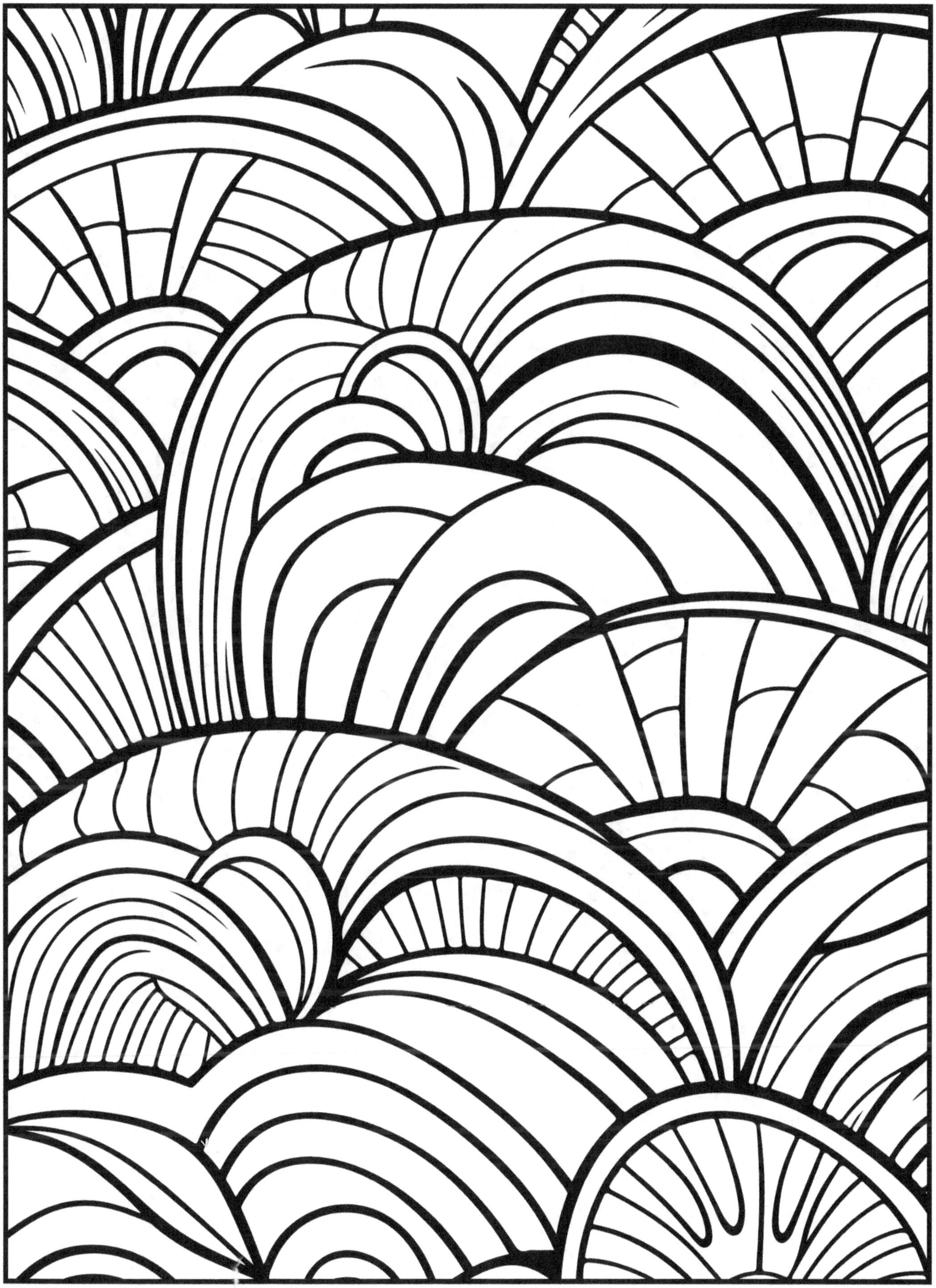

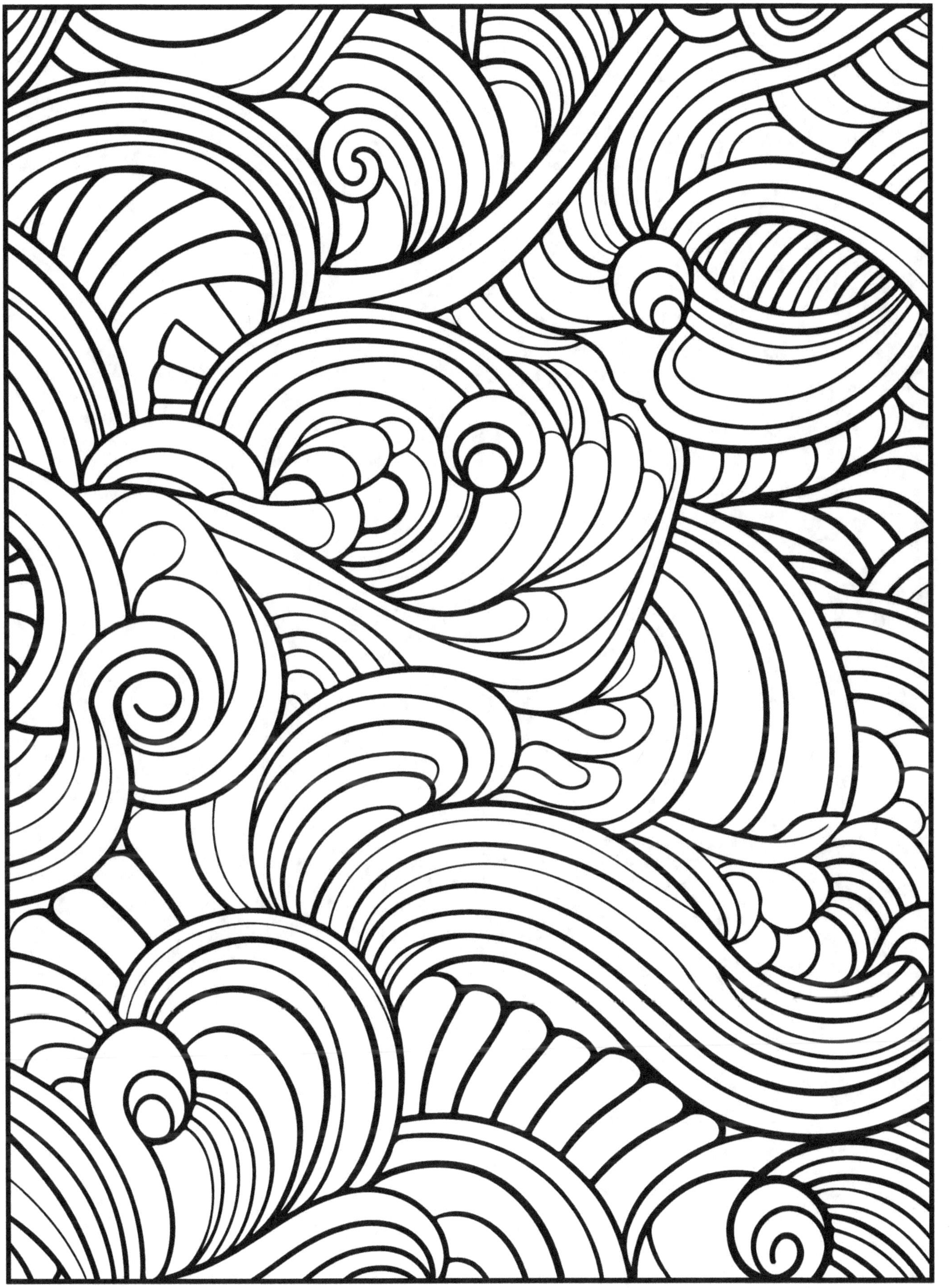

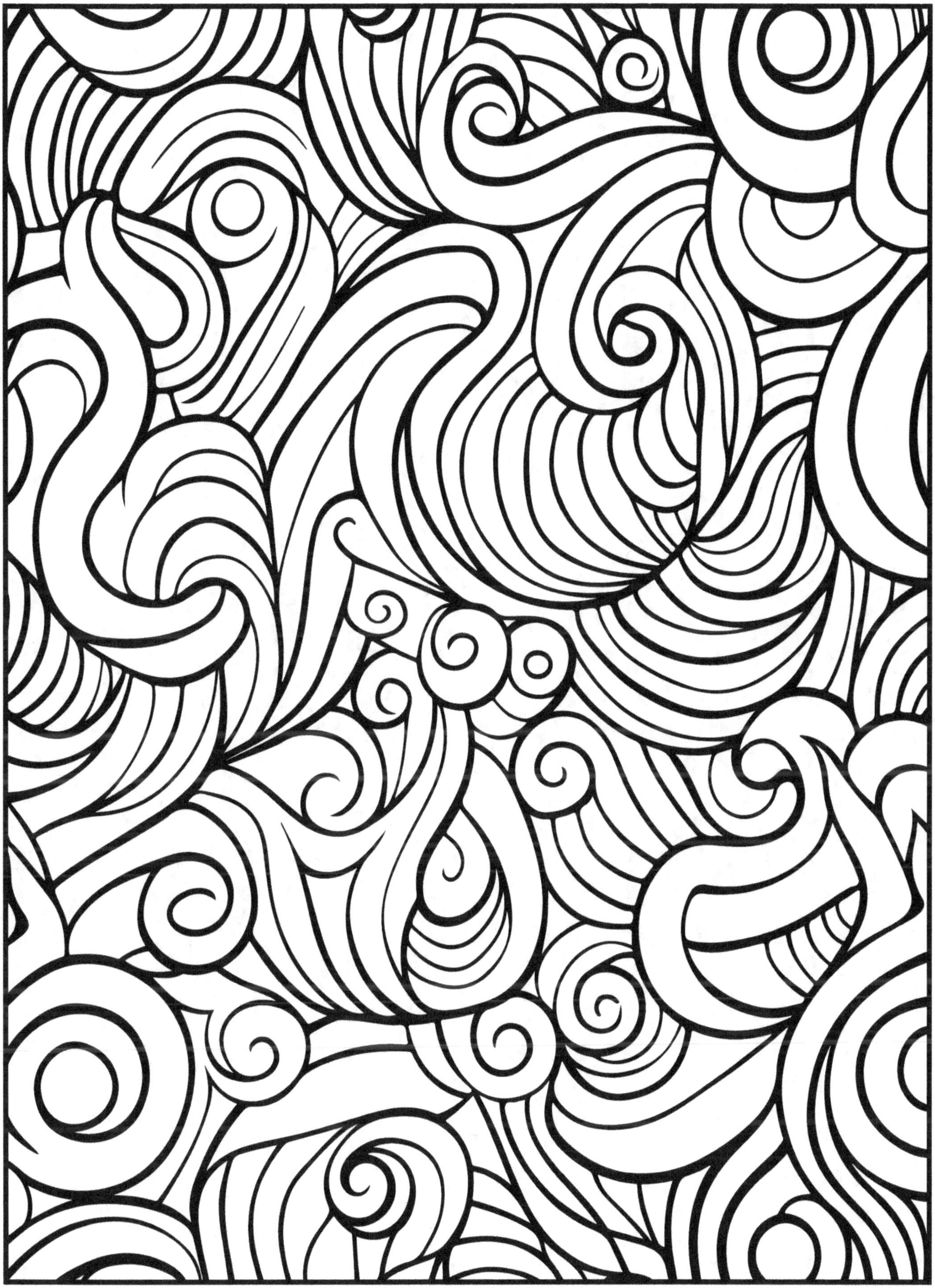

www.ingramcontent.com/pod-product-compliance
Lightning Source LLC
Chambersburg PA
CBHW082211220526
45470CB00010B/3125
* 9 7 9 8 3 2 7 5 6 1 2 8 1 *